Menander

The Grouch, Desperately Seeking Justice, Closely Cropped Locks, The Girl from Samos, The Shield

Edited by
David R. Slavitt *a n d* Palmer Bovie

PENN

University of Pennsylvania Press
Philadelphia

10 9 8 7 6 5 4 3 2 1

Published by
University of Pennsylvania Press
Philadelphia, Pennsylvania 19104-4011

Library of Congress Cataloging-in-Publication Data
Menander, of Athens
    [Works. English. 1998]
    Menander / edited by David R. Slavitt and Palmer Bovie
        p.   cm. — (Penn Greek drama series)
    Contents: The grouch—Desperately seeking justice—Closely cropped
locks—The girl from Samos—The shield.
    Includes bibliographic references (p.   ).
    ISBN 0-8122-3444-8 (cloth : alk. paper). —ISBN 0-8122-1652-0 (pbk :
alk. paper)
    1. Menander, of Athens—Translations into English.   2. Greek drama
(Comedy)—Translations into English.   I. Slavitt, David R., 1935–   .
II. Bovie, Smith Palmer.   III. Title.   IV. Series.
PA4246.E4   1998
882'.01—DC21   98-9966
                                                                     CIP

Contents

Introduction

Sheila D'Atri

Menander was born around 342 B.C. into a wealthy family and is said to have died at the age of 52. Theophrastus, a close friend, reports that Menander was a teacher of philosophy, and that his first play, the *Orge* ("Anger") was produced around 321 B.C., when Menander was 21 years old. His *Dyskolos* (here *The Grouch*), a copy of which we have today in a nearly complete form, won first prize at the Lenaea festival in 316/315. He is alleged to have had a mistress named Glykera ("Sweetheart"; the conventional name for a hetaira, or courtesan). Glykera is a character in several of Menander's plays, and an ancient mosaic, now in the Art Museum of Princeton University, shows and names Menander, Glykera, and Komodia ("The Spirit of Comedy").

Menander's facility in writing is illustrated by an ancient anecdote in which a friend says, "The Dionysia are coming. Haven't you composed your comedy?" Menander replies, "I *have* composed it, the plot is worked out. I only have to write the lines." The many papyrus texts found in Egypt from Hellenistic times to the seventh century A.D. attest to his lasting popularity. "O Menander, O Life!" runs the classical epigram, "Which of you has imitated the other?" The early Roman comedies of Plautus and Terence reflect a widespread familiarity with the plays of Menander, along with that of other New Comedy playwrights especially Diphilus and Philemon. Terence is even scolded for combining two plots from Menander in one play for comparison and balance—as Shakespeare did, for example, when he added the story of Gloucester and his two sons into the ancient legends of Lear and his daughters.

The style of New Comedy differs enormously from that of Old Comedy as written by Aristophanes in the fifth century B.C. Aristophanes wrote for a society that allowed political freedom and freedom of speech even in the midst of the Peloponnesian War (the great civil war of ancient Greece). But by the beginning of the fourth century democratic freedoms had been suppressed, and it would have been dangerous to broach political or religious questions, or to satirize prominent politicians openly. Comedy took a different turn, abandoning the elaborate and expensive choral passages, with their political commentary and fantastic costumes, for a quiet, matter-of-fact style becoming to the comedy of manners, nonpolitical and easily transferable to another time and place. By the late fourth century Middle Comedy favored as a predominant theme some form of mild travesty of mythology. This influence is seen in Plautus' *Amphitryo*, where the birth of Hercules is the result of Jupiter's transformation into Amphitryon and his seduction of Amphitryon's wife. Complicating the plot is Jupiter's helper Mercury, disguised as Amphitryon's slave Sosias, who has a meeting with the real Sosias that so rattles the slave that he goes off wondering if he has any identity at all. (The gods wear feathers in their caps so the audience can tell the difference!)

The theme of mistaken identity, which figures importantly in many of the comedies of Menander, derives not from Old Comedy but from the romantic melodramas of Euripides, which are even referred to and quoted in the Menandrian comedies, most notably in the *Aspis* (here *The Shield*) and the *Epitrepontes* (*Desperately Seeking Justice*). Many of these melodramas or tragicomedies of Euripides exist in fragmentary plays, but the plots of two surviving plays as well can be said to revolve around the problems of mistaken identity. One is *Iphigenia in Tauris*, where the hero Orestes is on the point of being slaughtered by a barbarian tribe when he and his supposedly sacrificed sister Iphigenia (now a priestess of the barbarians) recognize each other and escape together.

A similar theme appears in the *Ion*. The plot is familiar to readers of Menander: many years before the opening of the play, a girl was raped by Apollo and gave birth to a son. Afraid of her parents' reaction, she exposed the baby. Unbeknownst to her, Apollo rescues the child and has him brought up by the priestess at Delphi. At the time the play opens, the girl is grown, married, and unable to have a child. She and her husband go to the temple at Delphi to consult the god. The oracle leads the husband to believe that Ion is his own son; this brings about the mother's attempt to kill the boy and, when she fails, to Ion's attempt to kill his mother. Athena as "deus ex machina" resolves the crisis with the help of recognition tokens such as we see in the *Epitrepontes* (here *Desperately Seeking Justice*) and the *Perikeiromene* (*Closely Cropped Locks*).

The *Dyskolos*, found virtually complete less than forty years ago, does not use such a device, yet in the process of the drama the central character, Knemon, can be said to be brought to a recognition of his own character and its limitations. (Similarly, *King Oedipus* can be thought of as a recognition drama in that the progress of the plot follows Oedipus' discovery that he himself is the polluted being he seeks.) As a miserly misanthrope, Knemon thinks he has no need of other human beings, becoming furious at the thought of lending anything to a neighbor and responding with violence to friendliness. In the course of the play, in tribulation and mock-heroic disaster, he discovers how he is connected to humanity. As a consequence, he begins to show respect to the nearby shrine of the god Pan as well as to his fellow humans. By the end of the play, he allows his daughter to be married to a rich young man who has proved his true worth.

In the *Aspis* (*The Shield*) a young soldier is presumed to be dead because, in the heat of battle, another man picked up his shield: when the shield is discovered next to a corpse, a slave believes that his master is dead.

In the *Epitrepontes* a child who was exposed is found by a shepherd, who in turn gives it to a charcoal-burner and his wife. An argument arises when the shepherd wants to keep the items of embroidery and jewelry that were left with the child. The charcoal-burner argues from tragedy that the child's future may depend on his retaining the items that were left with him. The plot differs from a Euripidean situation in that the gods do not magically appear on high and resolve the problems of identity. In Menander's work, the gods may make a brief appearance as prologue, but only affect the action at a distance. The best candidate for divine influence is the goddess Chance.

The *Perikeiromene* has a complicated plot. A man whose wife has just died after giving birth to twins—a boy and a girl—exposes the babies. The foundlings are rescued by an old woman who gives up the boy and raises the girl, Glykera. Before she dies, she tells the girl her history and gives her the items (recognition tokens again!) found with her as an infant. The play opens when Polemon, a soldier and lover of the girl, in a jealous rage lops off her hair with his sword. Proud and angry, she leaves him, finding refuge with the adopted mother of her brother. At the end many reconciliations take place because the distinctive handiwork and ornaments serve to connect the missing father to his two children.

Samia is a character study, and its plot is an intricate exercise in maneuvering two fathers into accepting the romantic intentions and consequences of their children's relationship. One father, Demeas, is wealthy, generous, and kind. His mistress, Chrysis, is the girl from Samos, exiled to Athens after the Macedonian victory in 322 B.C. As a refugee and without Athenian citizenship, she could not marry Demeas although she lives with him. He has expressfully forbidden her to have a child. He does have a son, Moschion, who is in love with Plangon, the neighbor's daughter. When Plangon has a baby in the absence of the fathers, the baby is protected by Plangon's mother and then hidden and nursed by Chrysis, who had been pregnant but lost the child before the opening of the play. When Demeas overhears something that makes him think that Moschion is the father of Chrysis' child, he has the poor girl thrown out of his house and rages against the betrayal by his son and his mistress. Eventually the truth is unraveled, and the wedding of Plangon and Moschion is celebrated in the general reconciliation.

The texts of three of these plays are missing large portions. In the *Aspis* the first two acts and the beginning of the third are mostly intact, but only fragments—half-columns and assorted words—exist from the rest of the play. About half of the *Epitrepontes* is intact; the rest exists in mutilated condition, some parts clearer than others. The *Perikeiromene* is missing the opening scene (the papyrus begins early in the prologue) and the beginning and end of all the acts in varying degrees. Palmer Bovie and I agreed that what we wanted were readable texts, not translation interspersed with guesswork in italics. Therefore the decision was made to fill in the gaps with logical reconstruction from a general knowledge of Menander's intricate plot-lines and characterizations from these dramas from which a great deal survives, and also from the many plays that exist only in single scenes and short fragments.

The recovery of an almost complete text of the *Dyskolos* from the sands of Egypt in 1958 represents a major chapter in an ongoing modern miracle. However, we still have no clue as to the exact place and circumstances of the discovery of Papyrus Bodmer IV, which was written in the last half of the third century A.D. and contains the text of the play, a verse synopsis attributed to Aristophanes of Byzantium, and a cast of characters. This text has been matched with approximately forty lines which were previously known from quotations by ancient authors, and since 1958 four more fragments of five to nine lines each from two other papyrus finds have been added.

Other plays of Menander survive in part. Papyri found in 1905 contain half of *The Epitrepontes* and significant parts of *Perikeiromene* and *Samia*, and a nearly complete text of the *Samia* was found later. Since the discovery of the *Dyskolos*, Acts I and II and the beginning of Act III of *Aspis* were first published in 1969. Parts of *The Hated Man*, found on the back of papyrus finds containing a deed and a table of fractions, were published in 1965 and 1968. An excellent introduction to the papyri is Eric Turner's *Greek Papyri: An Introduction* (Princeton, N.J.: Princeton University Press, 1968).

Another word about the choruses. In the Old Comedy of Aristophanes, the chorus was a masterpiece of lyric as well as elaborate costume. In New Comedy, no choruses were written down—the text just indicates "ΧΟΡΟΥ" ("CHOROU," "of the chorus") to let us know that a group of drunken young men are about to enter the stage and sing a topical or contemporary drinking song. This device serves to divide the acts. I have taken the liberty of composing lyrics for the choruses, based on drinking songs and the poetry of previous generations. The art of comedy has calmed down but, still vibrant with emotion and intrigue, set itself the task of solving problems in recognizable human circumstances.

BIBLIOGRAPHY

Arnott, Peter. *Greek Scenic Conventions in the Fifth Century B.C.* Oxford: Clarendon Press, 1962.

Arnott, W. Geoffrey. "Menander: Discoveries Since the Dyskolos." *Arethusa* 3, 1 (1950): 59–60.

———. *Menander, Plautus, Terence.* Greece and Rome: New Surveys in the Classics 9. Oxford: Clarendon Press, 1975.

Bieber, Margarete. *The History of the Greek and Roman Theater.* Princeton, N.J.: Princeton University Press, 1961.

Blundell, John. *Menander and the Monologue.* Hypomnemata 59. Gottingen: Vandenhoeck and Ruprecht, 1980.

Fantham, Elaine. "Sex, Status, and Survival in Hellenistic Athens: A Study of Women in New Comedy." *Phoenix* 29 (1975): 44–74.

Flury, Peter. *Liebe und Liebessprache bei Menander, Plautus und Terence.* Heidelberg: C. Winder, 1968.

Gaiser, Konrad. "Die Plautinische Bacchides und Menanders Dis Exapaton." *Philologus* 114 (1970): 51–52.

Goldberg, Sander M. "Plautus' Epidicus and the Case of the Missing Original." *ETAPA* 108 (1978): 81–91.

———. *The Making of Menander's Comedy.* Berkeley: University of California Press, 1980.

Gomme, A. W. and F. H. Sandbach. *Menander: A Commentary.* Oxford: Oxford University Press, 1973.

The Grouch (Dyskolos)

Translated by
Sheila D'Atri

Translator's Preface

The Grouch or *Dyskolos* was produced in the winter of 316 B.C., when it won first prize at the Athenian festival of the Lenaea and Menander was in his mid-twenties. Five years earlier, he had won his first victory with the *Orge* (*Anger*), and although he was later admired as the greatest and most popular writer of New Comedy, there were only a few other plays— among over one hundred ascribed to him—that took first prize. He was born in the year 342/1 and grew up at a time when Athens was dominated by Macedon. The year the *Orge* was produced, a revolt inspired by Athens was crushed in both land and sea battles.

In the New Comedy of Menander and his contemporaries, freedom of expression was limited in comparison to the outspoken political and personal attacks with which we are familiar from the comedies of Aristophanes at the end of the fifth century. In a form of drama that has been called a comedy of manners, Menander was particularly adept at revealing character through dialogue and at coining memorable aphorisms within the dramatic context, much as Shakespeare did with Polonius and Claudius. Contemporary political or philosophical questions that arise in the context of the plays are of general topical interest, are not presented didactically, and are always subordinate to the characterization and the demands of the dramatic structure. For example, although at the time the *Dyskolos* was written, there was considerable discussion about the abuse of religious practices, when Knemon raves against hypocrisy and extravagance we must keep in mind that the speaker of these lines is a self-denying misanthropic miser whose own religious observances are grudging. The *Dyskolos* is a play that revolves around its title character, Knemon, the "dyskolos" (literally "dyspeptic") or "bad-tempered, intractable" old man. In antiquity, the play had the alternative title "The Misanthrope," a name often given to fourth-century comedies.

We are first introduced to Knemon indirectly, through the eyes of a slave he has terrified. He is described as a lonely figure on a barren rural hillside, gathering wild pears and reacting with violent fury when approached. The slave's terror at this meeting raises Knemon to an almost demonic force. This aspect of the old man is reinforced by his comments in his opening speech: he envies Perseus, not for his heroic qualities but for his ability to fly away from people and turn them to stone with the Medusa's head. The imagery suggests that his aversion to other people borders on the patho-logical. At first, he is completely unapproachable and unyielding, but, little by little, cracks appear in the armor. In a weak moment during Act III he complains of the "eremia" or emptiness of his life. His isolation is a prison even though it is self-imposed. The audience also begins to get an impres-sion of a creature whose bark is bigger than his bite when he threatens to force his old female slave Simiche to go down into the well. She is fright-ened, but in actuality Knemon descends himself.

The demonic force we see in Knemon at the beginning of the play is paralleled by the fierce and farcical behavior of the slave Getas and the cook Sikon at the end. The musical accompaniment lightens the atmosphere and lessens the impression of willful cruelty toward a sick old man. Knemon's discomforts are turned into ritual as Getas and Sikon force him to dance and badger him into joining the others who are sacrificing and celebrating in the shrine of Pan and the Nymphs. This way, the front-center of the stage becomes unified with the doings behind the entrance to the cave at the rear-center. As Sikon and Getas pester Knemon with his earlier responses, they force him to achieve at least a partial integration into a normal social world. Adding to the atmosphere produced by the music and ritual is the change of role slowly taking place in the tormentors. Sikon, the crudest character in the play, delivers lyrics in the most elevated mode as he describes the party in the cave.

Although most of the *Dyskolos* is written in iambic trimeters, the meter most approximating normal speech, Menander diverges in two places—during Knemon's "apologia," or defense of his way of life after his rescue, and in the scene at the end, played to the accompaniment of the flute. Getas and Sikon torment him in his misery as the characters disguised as wood-land creatures at the end of *The Merry Wives of Windsor* torment Falstaff.

Things even out. The request for a little stew-pot comes back to haunt Knemon, as they ask for huge and expensive paraphernalia. He is too weak to protest effectively and finally yields, just as, when he renounced his property, he gave away everything to his daughter and stepson. It is made clear that Knemon's self-sacrificing personality has been as hard on him as on anyone else. It is as if the demonic hold has been broken in the course of Knemon's fall into the well, especially in his recognition of the existence of altruism and the need for human interaction. Although at the end he is still a loner and does not want to join the sacrificers, yet he must celebrate, finally realizing that human beings cannot stand completely alone and that he was rescued by a stepson who had never received any good from him and expected nothing in return.

Menander allows Knemon to reveal himself directly in action and in a few very defining speeches, such as at his entrance when he describes a hostility of mythological proportions as he wishes for a Medusa's head. He slowly becomes less an ogre. In his next monologue, he complains of irreligious sacrifice in terms that are familiar in the writings of the peripatetic philosophers of the late fourth century, complaining about those who give to the god only the inedible parts of the sacrificial animal (the gall and the tail), claiming that the old-fashioned kind of sacrifice is the only true one— barley cakes, where the meal is totally given up to the gods. Menander has told us earlier that Knemon only greets the god Pan because he is afraid of retribution. He shows no religious interest himself, but clearly he begrudges luxury. The young lover Sostratos was rightly advised to take off his fancy cloak and do some farm work.

Indulgence disgusts Knemon and self-denial characterizes his way of life. Although his holdings are not small, he works his farmlands without help and with only the barest of tools. The rotten piece of rope that broke as the bucket was lowered into the well may have been his only rope, carefully saved. When he is desperate to find his mattock, we can guess that it is his only one. He works constantly, granting himself no pleasures (except perhaps for hot water), and expects the worst of everyone. Moreover (and Menander handles this motif with the greatest subtlety), Knemon sees himself as a victim, of people individually and of the whole world. When strangers come by and ask a question or (even worse) ask to borrow something, he abusively beats them with poles and leather straps and hurls pieces of sod and stones and even the sour wild pears he has been at great pains to gather. He calls the intruders man-eating animals, thinking that he is being tormented and that all he asks is to be left alone.

In a culture that prized hospitality (*xenia*) and where inhospitality was seen as a fundamentally irreligious act against Zeus Xenios, Knemon can be seen as a damned soul in need of rescue from himself. In the literary tradition, hospitality and transgressions against it have ancestral roots in the *Odyssey* and are an important theme in tragedy, comedy, and satyr play. The Cyclops eating his guests and Circe turning them into animals are primordial terrors, and it is images like these that Knemon recalls when he threatens to bite Getas' head off and gobble him down, and he expresses a wish to turn people into stone. When he says he has no salt and cannot lend any, this can be read also as an extreme of inhospitality, in that salt was basic to a household and salt was particularly mentioned to establish the depth of his refusal.

The *Dyskolos* can therefore be read as a kind of rescue drama in which the central character is literally rescued from a well into which he has fallen (to retrieve his broken-down possessions) and figuratively from the inhuman aspect of himself. Pan, in the prologue characterized him as an *apanthropos anthropos*—more than a misanthrope—an inhuman human being, a living contradiction in terms. Instead of being granted the power to turn people into inanimate objects, Knemon, a human figure lacking a vital aspect of the human anima or spirit, gained that within himself through the working of the god.

The young man in love, named Sostratos, is eager and impetuous and doesn't know what hit him. He has been picked by the god Pan as a reward to Knemon's daughter for her goodness and piety. Sostratos' manner of speech stands in contrast to that of the hard-working Gorgias, who is deliberate and full of homilies and "talks like a book."

As for the female characters, Simiche is not to be played seriously. She is a perfect parody of a tragic messenger bearing a tale of woe. Old women are frequently treated harshly in the comedies, but this one is hardly real—her presence jolts the action and changes the mood. The other women in the play reveal themselves as the men reveal their attitudes to them. Sostratos is contemptuous of his mother's habit of sacrificing, but he has no idea that his mother's dream was sent by Pan as is part of the god's plan for his own future. This dream will bring together all the participants and fulfill his fondest wishes. Getas has an impudent manner toward his mistress, but Sostratos' mother knows she is in charge, ignores the raillery, and demands that the job be done. The daughter is innocent and unspoiled and represents a sort of idealized heroine. She is not given any name in the papyrus; she is only identified by the label "Knemon's daughter." At her first appearance, her concern is for her old nurse and her manner is gracious, poised and noble. It has been noted that in her entrance with the water jug, Menander was creating a deliberate parody of the high-born but ignoble-looking Electra of Euripides. Even Knemon enjoys her company, talks to her, and really loves her. This capacity for love, which is made clear from the beginning, perhaps contains the germ of Knemon's salvation.

Generally, I have followed the Oxford text edited by F. H. Sandbach (Oxford: Clarendon Press, 1990), although I have occasionally used E. W. Handley's edition (Cambridge, Mass.: Harvard University Press, 1965) for the apportionment of lines as well as for his very valuable commentary.

POSTSCRIPT ON THE PAPYRI

The *Dyskolos* is the only example of Greek New Comedy that is virtually complete. The two most significant lacunae consist of a few missing lines easily bridged by stage directions. In the first instance, when Sikon is alone on stage as Knemon is being rescued from the well, four lines are missing and two are damaged at lines 650–56. In all probability, he is reporting and interpreting noises heard off stage. The second instance occurs at the beginning of Knemon's defense of his way of life at lines 703–10. By line 711 the meter has changed to the trochaic tetrameters that are used until the end of Act IV. One fragment quoted by an ancient author fits very well here, "I was in the habit of inflicting drudgery on myself."

Invenias etiam disiecti membra poetae.
(Still you may find the limbs of the dismembered poet.)
                                                    —Horace

Cast

PAN, the god, prologue speaker
SOSTRATOS, young man who has fallen in love
CHAIREAS, parasite, friend of Sostratos
PYRRHIAS, slave belonging to the family of Sostratos
KNEMON, the "dyskolos," the dyspeptic grouch
YOUNG GIRL, unmarried daughter of Knemon (no name given
    in the papyrus)
DAOS, slave belonging to Gorgias
GORGIAS, farmer, half-brother of Knemon's daughter by the
    same mother
SIKON, cook
GETAS, slave belonging to Sostratos' family
SOSTRATOS' MOTHER
SIMICHE, an old woman, Knemon's slave and nurse to his
    daughter
KALLIPPIDES, Sostratos' father
CHORUS of revelers
NONSPEAKING
    Plangon, Sostratos' sister
    Parthenis, a female piper
    Donax and Syrus, slaves
    Myrrhine, Knemon's wife and mother of Gorgias and the
        daughter
Another piper

*(The action takes place in Phyle, a village about thirteen miles from
Athens that was famous for a shrine to Pan and the Nymphs.
The actual shrine was on the side of a steep cliff; in the theater it
is represented by the opening to a cave in the center of the stage.
On the left is a farmhouse belonging to Knemon, the dyspeptic
misanthrope; on the right is another farmhouse belonging to
Gorgias and his mother. The spring of the Nymphs, where the
sacrifices take place, is inside the shrine. The audience cannot see
inside, so these actions will be reported. Next to one of the doors,
along the country lane that goes by the houses, is an altar to*

Apollo Agyieus, Apollo as the god of streets and roads. The
audience cannot see the well and dung-heap situated behind
Knemon's house or the lands farmed by Knemon and Gorgias,
but will imagine them as they are pointed out. The ridge where
Knemon is first seen picking wild pears is just off stage to the left.
Farther away, on the right, is the large farm owned by
Kallipides, Sostratos' father. The place has an air of desolation; it
is hilly, rocky, very difficult to farm, and mostly good for
hunting.)

ACT I

(In the early morning, the god Pan comes out of his shrine to deliver
the explanatory prologue to the audience.)

PAN

Let your imaginative forces work
to make this place appear as Phyle—
an Attic village where the celebrated shrine
from which I come belongs to those
who have the strength to farm the rocks.
The field here on my right belongs to Knemon,
a human lacking in humanity,
bilious toward everyone, detesting crowds.
"Crowds" do I say? He's lived a lengthy time
and hardly ever said a gracious word   10
to anyone. He's never first to say "hello,"
with one exception, and that's me,
his neighbor, Pan. He doesn't like it,
but he must. (I'm dangerous when crossed.)
This Knemon once was married to a widow
whose husband had just died and left her
with a tiny son. Yoked in one harness,
they lived by fighting through the days
and taking up the greater part of night

existing wretchedly. And then a daughter came,   20
and things got worse. When misery
was all there was, and life was harsh
and full of toil, she left and joined her son.
Here, in this neighborhood, he owned a little place,
where now he is his mother's sole support
(with barely enough). One loyal slave,
long in the family, is all the help they have.
This boy's quite grown by now.
His mind's advanced beyond his years.
Experience in living brought him up.   30
The old man and his daughter live alone
with an old female servant. Carrying wood,
digging, he works all the time.
Beginning with his wife and the neighbors
all the way to Cholargos, down there,
he hates every one of them. The girl
is innocent in all her ways—
not one thing ugly about her.
With pious care she tends the Nymphs
who share my shrine, and as she honors us   40
so are we moved to care for her.
There's a boy whose father farms a wealthy place,
worth many talents, right in this vicinity.
The city's where he lives, but now he's here
to hunt, and just by chance he's in this place
with his companion in the chase.
I've inspired him, made him mad for the girl:
That's the essence. If you want the rest,
watch if you wish—and you ought to wish it!
That youth I told you of is coming near,   50
intent on telling to his friend
these matters that we all might hear.
(Pan goes back to his shrine. Sostratos and a hunting companion, named
                Chaireas and called a parasite in the list of
                personae in the papyrus, come on stage from the
                farm belonging to Sostratos' father.)

CHAIREAS

> What are you saying? You saw a free-born girl
> putting garlands on the local Nymphs—
> and right away you're in love?

SOSTRATOS

> Right away.

CHAIREAS

> That's fast. When you started out today
> did you plan to fall in love?

SOSTRATOS

> You're mocking me,
> but I am really wretched, Chaireas.   60

CHAIREAS

> It's not that I don't believe you.

SOSTRATOS

> That's why I'm taking you into my heart.
> I also think of you as practical.

CHAIREAS

> That's the way I am, Sostratos.
> Suppose a hetaira has captured a friend.
> Right away I grab her, get drunk,
> burn down the house! Don't listen to reason!
> Before you discover who she is,
> you've got to try your luck.
> Slow-going makes you burn for a girl,   70
> and a quick start means a quick finish.
> But if you mean marriage with a free-born female,
> then I'm a different sort of friend.
> I make inquiries about her family,
> finances and style. It's permanent

arrangements that we're talking here.
I leave a future record for my friend.

SOSTRATOS
   That's well and good,
   but not very pleasing.

CHAIREAS
   But even in your case we should   80
   give the facts a thorough hearing.

SOSTRATOS
   At dawn I sent out Pyrrhias
   from home, but not to hunt—

CHAIREAS
   To whom?

SOSTRATOS
   To her father. To meet with
   the person in charge, whoever he is.

CHAIREAS
   Heracles! What are you saying?

SOSTRATOS
   I made a mistake. Missions like these
   Aren't for slaves. It isn't easy
   to know what succeeds, when someone's in love.   90
   It's been quite some time since he's been gone,
   and I've been wondering—I said to him—
   "Get right back home, and tell me here,
   where I am waiting, what I want to know."
(They are suddenly interrupted by a terrified Pyrrhias dashing onto the
               stage from the left. He is out of breath and dazed
               as if he has just encountered a malevolent spirit
               of superhuman force.)

PYRRHIAS
> Make room! Watch out! Get off the road!
> A crazy man is chasing me—he's mad!

SOSTRATOS
> What's this all about, my lad?

PYRRHIAS
> Save yourselves!

SOSTRATOS
> What's this?

PYRRHIAS
> I'm pelted with clods, with sod, with stones.   100
> I'm dead.

SOSTRATOS
> Pelted? Where to now, you miserable wretch?

PYRRHIAS *(trying to escape across to the right)*
> Is he still coming after me?

SOSTRATOS *(holding him back)*
> By Zeus, he's not!

PYRRHIAS
> He was, I thought.

SOSTRATOS
> What are you saying?

PYRRHIAS
> Let's clear out of here, I'm begging!

SOSTRATOS
> Where?

PYRRHIAS

    Away from his door, as far as we're able.

    Some son of Distress, a man possessed   110

    by blackness of bile and dreadful demons

    lives there. You sent me to a man

    who is big trouble. I've broken my toes

    falling over all those rocks.

SOSTRATOS

    Has he been drinking, coming here like this?

CHAIREAS

    His wits are wandering, that's clear.

PYRRHIAS

    By Zeus, I swear it, Sostratos,

    I'd rather die! Watch out somehow.

    I can't go on; I'm out of breath.

    I knocked on the door and asked for the master,   120

    A beaten-down old woman came—

    she stood right here, where I am now

    and showed me where he was

    up on the hill collecting sour pears.

(Pyrrhias is frantic. His encounter with the old man has made him

                 sound like an incompetent fool. Chaireas and

                 Sostratos find the story hard to believe since they

                 have not yet seen Knemon.)

CHAIREAS *(sarcastically)*

    What excitement!

PYRRHIAS

    What's that, you lucky dog? But as for me,

    I took some steps upon his bit of land,

    and while a good way off, in friendly fashion,

    Put out my hand in greeting as I spoke.

    "I've come on business, sir," I said.   130

"On your behalf, I've hurried here."
Right away, he says, "Damn you, are you
spying on my place?" Then he
picked up some sod and threw it in my face.

CHAIREAS *(incredulously)*
　　Go to hell!

PYRRHIAS
　　While this was going on, I shut my eyes,
　　and said, "I hope Poseidon gets you,"
　　when next he grabbed a pointed pole
　　and really cleaned me up with it.
　　He said,"What business could there be,"   140
　　of some concern to you and me?"
　　"Can't you find a public road?" he screamed.

CHAIREAS
　　Without a doubt, you're describing
　　a farmer who's out of his mind.

PYRRHIAS
　　Here's how it ends: I ran away
　　and he chased me, first around the hill,
　　at least two miles, and then below
　　into these bushes, throwing clods and stones
　　and then the pears when nothing else was there.
　　A rotten business, an absolutely   150
　　damned old man. I beg you, find another place.

SOSTRATOS
　　That's the way that cowards talk.

PYRRHIAS
　　You've no idea what path you walk.
　　He'll gobble us up.

CHAIREAS
  Perhaps at this moment he's suffering.
  It seems to me now, Sostratos, that we
  can wait awhile. For you should know,
  in business, it's more practical
  to wait until the moment's opportune.

PYRRHIAS
  Very sensible.   160

CHAIREAS
  Poor farmers are prickly, He's not alone;
  It's all of them. At dawn, tomorrow,
  since I know the house, I'll go alone.
  And now it's best you wait at home.
  That's the way to play it.
(Having decided to his own satisfaction what would be best, Chaireas
  departs without waiting for an answer. Sostratos
  then turns his attention to his slave after deciding
  that Chaireas is of no use to him.)

PYRRHIAS *(happy to have Chaireas take care of things)*
  That's what we should do.

SOSTRATOS *(thinking Chaireas has failed him)*
  That's an excuse he's gladly seized upon.
  It was immediately clear
  he didn't want to come with me,
  and didn't approve of my marriage plans.   170
(turning furiously to Pyrrhias)
  And as for you, you lowest of the low,
  I hope the gods destroy you.

PYRRHIAS *(innocently)*
  How have I injured you, Sostratos?

SOSTRATOS
    It's clear you've caused some damage to his place,
    or stole—

PYRRHIAS
    I stole?

SOSTRATOS
    Why would someone beat you if you did nothing wrong?

PYRRHIAS
    He's here, that man himself! O best of masters,
    now I'll take me off, and you can talk to him.
(Pyrrhias makes his escape. Sostratos on stage alone starts his monologue.
                As he is speaking, he notices Knemon appear at the
                left, coming from the ridge. By the time his speech
                is finished, Sostratos has moved as far away as
                he can from Knemon's house, while Knemon is
                standing in the middle of the stage, ready to begin
                his comments to the spectators.)

SOSTRATOS *(to himself and answering the absent Pyrrhias)*
    I can't! I never can persuade a soul   180
    no matter what I talk about.
    And how can I address a man like him?
    That's no philanthropist I'm looking at.
    By Zeus, he's serious! I'll slip aside
    a little from the door. That's better.
    How he shouts, while walking all alone!
    He must be mad, it seems to me—
    I'm frightened, by Apollo and the gods.
    (Shouldn't a person tell the truth?)

KNEMON
    Well, didn't Perseus have double-luck?   190
    First, the wings—he never had to meet

with people walking on the ground.
And then he had some sort of property
which turned the mob of nuisances to stone.
That's what I want! They'd be plentiful
everywhere—human statues made of stone.
By Asclepius, my life is now
unlivable. They're talking,
trespassing, crossing my land.
I suppose, by Zeus, I waste my time   200
standing by the side of the road!
I don't work that bit of field:
those people coming by have chased me off,
and now they follow me up to the hill-tops.
A multi-multitudinous mob!
Good grief! Another one of them
is standing right beside our door!

SOSTRATOS *(aside)*
    Will he really strike at me?

KNEMON *(aside)*
    A quiet place is nowhere to be found.
    You can't even plan to hang yourself in peace.   210

SOSTRATOS *(aside)*
    Can it be me enraging him?
(to Knemon)
    I'm waiting here for someone, sir, it was agreed—

KNEMON *(ignoring him)*
    What did I say? Is this the stoa
    or the local shrine for rendezvous?
    Whenever there's a man you wish to see,
    arrange to meet them all beside my door.
    Certainly, construct an assembly-room,
    if that's what you have in mind!

Why not a council-chamber? I'm accursed!
The evil is abusive insolence,   220
as it appears to me.
(Knemon exits, going angrily into his house.)

SOSTRATOS

I can't be casual about this job.
Real effort is required here.
That's clear, but shall I go for Getas,
who's my father's slave? By the gods, I will!
He's hot stuff, with lots of experience
in all sorts of things. He'll beat off his bile.
I don't approve of long delays:
why, even in a single day,
lots could happen. Oh, there's noise at the door!   230
(Young girl, Knemon's daughter, enters.)

GIRL

Alas, for all my sufferings;
and what shall I do now? My nurse,
while lifting up the jar,
dropped the well-ropes in the well.

SOSTRATOS *(aside, thinking only of the appeal of his beloved)*
O Father Zeus, Apollo the healer,
beloved Dioscuri—unbeatable beauty!

GIRL

Father gave me orders coming in
to make the water hot.

SOSTRATOS *(overwhelmed by her)*
Amazing!

GIRL

If he discovers this, he'll treat her   240
like a criminal. I have no time to talk.

O dearest Nymphs, you've got to take it on.
But I'm ashamed to go inside
if there are people making sacrifice—

SOSTRATOS
    Just give it to me and right away
    I'll dip the jug and bring it up.

GIRL
    Yes, by the gods, and quickly too!

SOSTRATOS *(to himself as he goes into the shrine)*
    She's a natural aristocrat
    although her look is countrified.
    O gods deserving deepest reverence,   250
    what can save me now?

GIRL
    Dear me, who's banging at the door?
    Can that be father coming out?
    I'll catch some blows if he catches me out.

DAOS *(speaking to Gorgias' mother inside as he comes on stage from the other
        house)*
    I'm slaving and serving forever here
    while he's out there digging alone.
    I've got to go and help him out.
    O cursed Poverty! How have we happened
    on such an intimate relationship?
    Why has your constant presence   260
    settled in our house?

SOSTRATOS *(returning)*
    Take the jar.

GIRL *(from the door of her house)*
    Bring it here.

DAOS
  Whatever is this man after?

SOSTRATOS
  Be well! Take care of your father.
(to himself)
  Oh, my! O Sostratos, stop complaining.
  It will be all right.

DAOS *(aside)*
  What will be all right?

SOSTRATOS *(still to himself)*
  Don't worry, do as you planned—get Getas—
  tell him everything and bring him back.   270
(He goes offstage.)

DAOS *(alone)*
  Is something ugly going on?
  I'm not the least bit pleased.
  When a boy is waiting on a girl,
  corruption's close. But, Knemon, as for you—
  I hope the gods destroy you totally.
  You've left that innocent and harmless girl
  alone in this deserted place,
  with no protection anywhere.
  That's why he came by! Finding out,
  he slipped away and thought he'd try his luck.   280
  Fast as I can, I'll let her brother know.
  We'll watch out on her behalf.
  I believe I will start on it now—
  for here's a group of followers of Pan.
  I see they're looking somewhat drunk,
  so I think I'm better off away.
*(Chorus of revelers comes on stage, singing a lighthearted paean to Pan
            and providing the choral performance sung
            between the acts.)*

ACT II

(Daos and Gorgias are alone on stage. Gorgias, hearing about Sostratos' arrival at the farm, criticizes Daos for not dealing more forcefully with the situation.)

GORGIAS

Was this an insignificant affair
that you could handle carelessly?

DAOS

How is that?

GORGIAS

You should have told him, whoever he was,   290
as soon as you saw him come forward,
by Zeus, that you'd better never,
ever see him again acting like that.
But you kept off, as if this business
was somebody else's concern.
It isn't possible to run away
from family responsibility.
My sister's our concern, although her father
wishes it were otherwise. Don't imitate
dyspeptic dispositions.   300
If she falls victim to some shame,
disgrace would also come to me.
From the outside, no one ever knows
who is to blame. They only see results.

(They walk toward Knemon's house.)

DAOS

Gorgias, my friend, I'm afraid
of that old man. If he catches me
near his door, he'll hang me on the spot.

GORGIAS

He's certainly intractable,
always adversarial. How could someone

force him to improve or use persuasion?   310
The law prevents our use of force,
And persuasion's ruled out by his nature.

DAOS

Hold on a bit—we haven't come in vain—
Just as I said, he's turning back again.

GORGIAS

The one in the fancy cloak?
Have you been speaking of HIM?

DAOS

He's the one.

GORGIAS

I can see from his looks, he's a villain.

SOSTRATOS *(entering, unaware of Daos and Gorgias; aside)*
I couldn't find Getas, he wasn't in.
My mother's off to sacrifice   320
to some divinity—I don't know who
every day she's doing some such thing.
She circles round the entire district
making sacrifice, and Getas was sent
to contract for a cook. I said good-bye
to sacrifice, and here I am again.
I think I'll get rid of this going around
and do my talking for myself.
I'll knock at the door, although it may be, I'll never take counsel
        again.

GORGIAS

My lad, would you please wait a while? I've something serious
        to say.   330

SOSTRATOS
　　My pleasure, certainly.

GORGIAS
　　For humankind, I do believe,
　　for those with luck and those unfortunate,
　　change and limitation is the rule.
　　The one with luck remains as such,
　　flourishing throughout his life,
　　as long as fortune can be borne
　　without injustice. But when THAT's there
　　and leading him by all the goods he owns,
　　it's then, I think, all changes for the worse.　　　　340
　　Yet, as for those who do not have enough,
　　in difficulty, doing nothing wrong,
　　bearing up with all nobility,
　　perhaps, in time, they'll find some credit
　　and share in better expectations.
　　What am I trying to say?
　　Although you're rich, don't trust in it,
　　and don't despise us just because we're poor.
　　Let anyone who's watching see
　　you're worth enduring fortune.　　　　350

SOSTRATOS
　　I appear to do something out of place?

GORGIAS
　　I believe you're eager for a cheap trick—
　　planning to persuade a free-born girl
　　to fall, or else you're waiting
　　for an opportune time
　　for an action worth multiple deaths.

SOSTRATOS
　　By Apollo!

GORGIAS

    Certainly, it isn't just
    that at your ease you work your wickedness
    on us who have no leisure for such things.   360
    Know, then, that a poor man harmed
    is the most ferocious of all.
    At first he's piteous, then it's outrage
    he's suffered, not merely injustice.

SOSTRATOS

    May all go well for you, dear boy,
    But hear me out a bit.

DAOS *(to Gorgias)*

    Great going sir! Lots of luck to you!

SOSTRATOS *(to Daos)*

    As for you, babbler, stifle yourself—
    in this place, I saw a certain girl.
    I love her. If you call that injury—   370
    then perhaps I'm in the wrong.
    Can anyone say more? Except it's not
    for her I've come—I want to see her father.
    I'm free-born and sufficiently rich
    to marry her without a dowry.
    I pledge to love her perpetually.
    If I have come with malice on my mind,
    or wished to plot intrigues in secrecy,
(pointing to the statue of Pan on stage)
    may this Pan, together with the Nymphs,
    strike me dead beside the house.   380
    I'm really disturbed, I hope you know,
    if that's the way I seem to you.

GORGIAS

    Maybe I've spoken more than I should—
    don't get yourself upset—you've changed my mind.

Now I'm your friend. I'm no stranger,
but her brother (we have the same mother).
Best of men, that's why I've spoken this way.

SOSTRATOS
And now, by Zeus, you'll be useful!

GORGIAS
What do you mean useful?

SOSTRATOS
I see you have a noble character.   390

GORGIAS
I don't want to send you off empty.
No pretexts—but the plain truth.
The father of this girl—he's just—
like no one else. There never was
a man like him, and no one living's like him now.

SOSTRATOS
That vicious man? I've seen him here.

GORGIAS
An absolute excess of abuse!
His holdings (not so small—two talents worth)
he farms alone, without a laborer
to share the work: no household slave   400
or paid employee from the neighborhood,
no neighbor either, just himself alone.
Happiness to him is seeing no one near.
Mostly he works with his daughter around.
To her alone he cares to speak,
but not to any other easily.
He says he'll never let her marry
until he finds a bridegroom just like him.

SOSTRATOS
What you mean is never.

GORGIAS
And that's why, my good friend,   410
if you take pains to work at this,
you'll work in vain. Leave it to us
who have no choice, to bear with him.

SOSTRATOS
By the gods, have you never loved someone?

GORGIAS
It's not for me, my friend.

SOSTRATOS
How's that? Who's preventing you?

GORGIAS
Calculating the troubles I have
gives me no time to rest.

SOSTRATOS
You've never been, I think.
Your speech shows no experience in things like this.   420
You exhort me to withdraw.
The decision is no longer mine—
it is the god's.

GORGIAS
Although you're doing us no harm,
you're only needlessly distressed.

SOSTRATOS
Not if I can win the girl!

GORGIAS
>But you won't. Follow me. Attempt to ask.
>He's farming near us in a wooded glen.

SOSTRATOS
>How will it go?

GORGIAS
>I'll throw in a word about a marriage   430
>to the girl. (That's a thing I'd gladly see!)
>Right away he'll start complaining
>about everyone, criticizing
>the way they live. When he gets sight of you
>looking luxurious, he won't even look!

SOSTRATOS
>Now—is he there?

GORGIAS
>No, but in a little while,
>It's out he'll come on his accustomed path.

SOSTRATOS
>Are you saying he'll bring the girl along?

GORGIAS
>It may work out that way.   440

SOSTRATOS
>Go ahead, I'm ready.

GORGIAS
>The way you talk!

SOSTRATOS
>I'm begging you, be on my side!

GORGIAS
But in what way?

SOSTRATOS
What way? Let's go ahead to where you said.

DAOS
What now? While we are working,
do you plan to hang around
wearing that fancy cloak?

SOSTRATOS
Why shouldn't I?

DAOS
He'll pelt you with pieces of sod   450
and call you a lazy pest. You must
dig along with us. Maybe then he might
perhaps hold off and hear a word,
thinking you lead a poor farmer's life.

SOSTRATOS
I'm ready to do as I'm told. Go on!
(He takes off the cloak, and can now work unencumbered in only a short
tunic.)

GORGIAS
Why do you force yourself
to suffer such distress?

DAOS *(aside)*
What I wish is that today
we get as much as possible
accomplished. Maybe at the same time,   460
he'll break his back and stop annoying us.

SOSTRATOS

> Bring out the two-pronged hoe!

DAOS

> Go on, take mine. Meanwhile I'll rebuild the wall.
> That also must be done.

SOSTRATOS

> Hand it over—you've saved me!

DAOS

> I'm setting out, my man, you follow there.

SOSTRATOS

> So that's the way it is. I must die trying,
> or win her and live!

GORGIAS

> If you are speaking as you're thinking,
> I wish you luck.   470

SOSTRATOS

> Great honored gods! If you believe
> those things you said would turn me off,
> you're wrong—I'm doubly keen.
> If this girl hasn't been reared
> among women, and knows nothing
> of the evils of this life,
> and hasn't been terrified
> by the imaginings of some aunt or nurse,
> but with freedom of spirit, somehow,
> by a harsh father detesting wicked ways—   480
> Isn't she a specially lucky find?
> But—this hoe must weigh two hundred pounds!
> It's killing me! Can't soften now—
> that I've set myself to work at it.

SIKON *(coming on stage with the sheep)*
  A sheep like this one doesn't come along
  every day. Damn it to hell!
  If I carry it up in the air,
  it grabs a branch in its mouth
  and gobbles the fig-leaves from the tree.
  I've got to drag it off by force.   490
  If you set it on the ground, it won't move.
  The opposite takes place. I am the cook—
  and I'm the one in shreds,
  dragging along the road.
  Happily, here's the temple to the Nymphs,
  where we will sacrifice. Greetings Pan!
  Hey boy! You—Getas—why are you hanging behind?

GETAS *(entering, loaded down with cushions and cookery)*
  Those damnable women loaded me up
  with enough for four donkeys.

SIKON
  It looks like a mob is arriving.   500
  That's a lot of bedding you're bearing!

GETAS
  What now?

SIKON
  Lean those things over there.

GETAS
  Ok. If she should see
  Paianian Pan in her sleep,
  that's where we'd go, I know,
  right for the sacrifice!

SIKON
  Who saw something asleep?

GETAS
> Hey man, don't beat on me.

SIKON
> Tell me anyway, Getas, who?   510

GETAS
> My mistress.

SIKON
> But what, by the gods?

GETAS
> You'll destroy me! It seemed that Pan—

SIKON *(pointing to the statue on stage)*
> This one over here?

GETAS
> This one.

SIKON
> What was he doing?

GETAS
> The master, Sostratos—

SIKON
> A really refined young man!

GETAS
> Was putting shackles all about him.

SIKON
> By Apollo!   520

GETAS

> Then giving him a leather vest
> and a two-pronged hoe, he ordered him to dig
> in some neighbor's land.

SIKON

> Unbelievable!

GETAS

> Because of this we sacrifice,
> to turn the nightmare into something good.

SIKON

> Now I've got it! Pick up that stuff again,
> and carry it inside. We've got to have
> the cushions set up right
> and everything else in order.   530
> Nothing should get in the way
> when they're ready to sacrifice.
> Here's to luck! And lift those eyebrows up,
> you triple-miserable wretch.
> Today I'll gorge you to your taste!

GETAS

> I've always been quick to praise your craft.
> But YOU, I don't trust.

(They go off into the shrine. Chorus enters with another song.)

ACT III

> *(Knemon comes out of his house, calling back to Simiche inside. He
> is getting ready to start some farm-work, but his plans are
> interrupted by the arrival of Sostratos' mother, Plangon, and
> Parthenis, who have come to sacrifice at the shrine of Pan.)*

KNEMON

> Old woman, once you bar the door,
> don't open it for anyone

until I come again. By then   540
I think it should be quite dark.

MOTHER OF SOSTRATOS
Plangon—go faster—our sacrifice
ought to be finished by now!

KNEMON *(unseen and unheard by the others)*
What rotten business is this?
A crowd! Why don't you go where the crows
can pick your bones?

MOTHER *(to the flute-girl)*
Parthenis! Pipe Pan's melody!
They say that no one should approach
this god in silence.

GETAS *(long familiar with his mistress' sacrifices)*
By Zeus—you got here safe enough!   550
Heracles! How wearing! We've been sitting
forever and hanging around.

MOTHER
Has all been set in order for us?

GETAS
Yes, by Zeus—at least the sheep—
it almost died waiting.

MOTHER
You wretch—it won't wait around
till you've the time. Now all of you go in—
make ready the basket, the lustral water,
the sacrificial cakes. Why are you gaping?
Have you been struck by thunder?   560
*(Sostratos' mother exits into the house. Getas meanwhile sees Knemon
coming out of his house looking furious.)*

KNEMON
Damn you pests to deepest hell!
They're forcing laziness on me—
I just can't leave an unprotected house!
These Nymphs are a curse across my door—
I think I'll build another house,
tearing this one down.
Look how those burglars sacrifice!
They're bringing bedding and bottles of wine—
not goods for the gods—but good for them!
What's holy is incense and barley-cake.   570
This, when set upon the fire,
the god takes totally. The other things—
the inedible gall and the tail—
that's what they offer to the gods
while they gulp down the rest.
Old woman—quickly—open the doors!
I think we should work on the inside chores.
(Knemon goes back into his house.)

GETAS *(talking to servants in the shrine)*
The little stew-pot you say you forgot?
You're sleeping it off! What can be done?
I think we've got to trouble the neighbors   580
of the god.
(knocks on Knemon's door)
Slave! By the gods!
Nowhere is there a more miserable
mob of serving-girls. Hey, slaves!
It's only screwing that they understand!
My fine fellows! And if someone sees,
why, then they slander someone else. Slave!
What the hell is this? Servants!
No one is in. Oh! Someone's racing up!
(Knemon appears at the door.)

KNEMON
Why are you attached to my door? Tell me, you miserable boor. 590

GETAS
> Don't bite off my head!

KNEMON
> I'll do just that, by Zeus,
> and then I'll devour you alive.

GETAS
> You won't—by the gods!

KNEMON
> Is there some sort of legal covenant
> binding me to you, you godforsaken pest?

GETAS
> No bond. I haven't come with witnesses to ask that a debt be
> > repaid.
> I'm only requesting a small stew-pot.

KNEMON
> Stew-pot?

GETAS
> Stew-pot.   600

KNEMON
> You whipping-post, do you suppose
> I make it a habit to sacrifice cows?

GETAS
> I don't think you'd offer a snail.
> I hope you prosper, my good man.
> The women suggested I knock and ask
> so that's what I did. There isn't any.
> When I return, that's the statement I'll make.
> O honored gods, this man's a gray-haired snake.
(Getas returns to the shrine.)

KNEMON *(alone)*

    Man-killing beasts! As if I were a friend—
    no one hesitates to knock. If I should catch   610
    a man advancing to this door of ours,
    if I don't make a warning out of him
    to everyone around, then think of me
    as just one of the crowd! I don't know
    who he was, but this time he lucked out.
(Knemon returns inside his house and Sikon emerges from the shrine. He
begins by speaking to Getas, who is inside.)

SIKON

    Damn you to hell! So he was abusive?
    Probably you were foul-mouthed first.
    Some people don't understand how to ask—
    but I invented the art!
    I supply for tens of thousands in this town.   620
    You've got to be a bit of a flatterer—
    if an older man opens the door,
    I call him "Father" or "Pop";
    an older woman I call "Mother";
    if it's a woman of middle-age,
    it's "Sister" or "Milady";
    if one of the younger slaves, "My good man."
    But you can go hang yourself stupidly, you say "Boy" or Slave,"
    where I say "Papa, a word with you, please."
(He knocks and Knemon appears.)

KNEMON

    Are YOU back?   630

SIKON

    How's that?

KNEMON

    You're provoking me purposely.
    Didn't I say "Keep away from my door?"
    Woman, hand me the whip!

SIKON
>   Never! Let me go.

KNEMON
>   Let go?

SIKON
>   My good man, truly, by the gods!

KNEMON
>   Get back here.

SIKON
>   May Poseidon grant you—

KNEMON
>   Still chattering?   640

SIKON
>   I came to request an earthen casserole.

KNEMON
>   I have no earthen casserole,
>   nor do I possess an axe, nor salt,
>   nor vinegar—only nothing!
>   I've stated it simply to everyone near
>   Don't approach!

SIKON
>   You never said it to me.

KNEMON
>   Now I'm saying it.

SIKON
>   Yes, with brute force! Couldn't you tell me
>   where one might go to ask for one?   650

KNEMON
  Didn't I say? Will you still jabber at me?

SIKON
  A grand fare-well.

KNEMON
  I don't want any "fare-well" from you.

SIKON
  Fare badly then.

KNEMON
  Oh, what incurable ills!
(Knemon exits into his house, leaving Sikon on stage.)

SIKON
  He's furrowed me into strips of sod!
  So that's what you get for polite requests!
  Some difference, by Zeus!
  Should one approach another door?
  If they're all so ready with fighting-gloves here,   660
  It would be difficult. Maybe it's best
  to roast all the meat. That's how it appears.
  Anyway, I've got a pan.
  Good-bye to Phyle—I'll use what's at hand.
*(He returns to the shrine. Shortly afterward an exhausted Sostratos
                          enters.)*

SOSTRATOS
  Whoever is lacking in troubles,
  Let him go hunting in Phyle.
  Oh, multiple miseries,
  since I have a back and neck and hips—
  to put it briefly—my whole body hurts.
  I fell into this job like a strong young man;   670

lifting the hoe like a laborer,
I struck it deep. I laid it on
with diligence, but not for long—
then I'd turn and look, in case it was the time
for the old man to come with the girl,
and then, by Zeus, I took hold of my hip,
secretly at first, and after quite a while,
my spine was bent. I was quietly
turning to timber. The sun was burning,
and Gorgias, looking over, saw me   680
bending slightly up like a swing-beam
and then going heavily down
with all my body striking it.
"Young fellow," he said, "That man,
it seems, will not come now." I answered,
"So what should we do? Keep watch tomorrow
and let today go by?" Then Daos came
as my successor to the spade.
The first assault is done. I've come
here, though I can't say why, by the gods.   690
Of its own accord, this business
drags me to this place.
*(Getas appears at the door of the shrine, trying to get the smoke out of his
eyes. He shouts back inside at Sikon.)*

GETAS

What's the trouble now? Do you think,
my man, I've sixty hands? I kindle the coal,
cut up the guts, wash, and carry to and fro
and at the same time I'm kneading the dough.
I hand this implement around and then—
I'm blinded by the smoke. At times like these,
I think I'm the donkey at the feast.

SOSTRATOS

    Slave! Getas!   700

GETAS
Someone's calling me?

SOSTRATOS
I am.

GETAS *(still blinded)*
And who are you?

SOSTRATOS
You don't see me?

GETAS
I see you now—Master!

SOSTRATOS
Tell me what YOU are doing here.

GETAS
What? We've just made the sacrifice
and now we're preparing the morning meal.

SOSTRATOS
Is Mother here?

GETAS
For quite some time.   710

SOSTRATOS
And Father?

GETAS
We expect him. You can go inside.

SOSTRATOS
After I've run a little errand.
Somehow, the timing's fine for sacrifice.

I'll invite this young man, going just as I am,
and also his slave. If they share
in the offerings, then in the future,
they'll be more useful allies of ours
regarding the marriage.

GETAS

What are you saying? You're planning to go   720
and invite some people to share the meal?
For my sake, let there be three thousand!
I've known it for a long time—
I won't get a taste of anything. Hardly!
Bring everyone. You've sacrificed
a lovely victim—really worth seeing.
As for these women—they're sophisticates—
but would they give me something? No.
By Demeter, not even bit of coarse salt!

SOSTRATOS

Getas, today it will go well—   730
I'll prophesy myself, O Pan—
and always pray while passing you.
I'll be a friend to all mankind.
(*Sostratos exits, looking for Gorgias and Daos.*)

SIMICHE (*dashing tragically out of the house*)
Oh, woe is me! Oh, woe is me! Oh, woe is me!

GETAS

Go to Hell! That's the old man's woman coming up.

SIMICHE

What will become of me?
Wanting to get the pail from the well,
without the master finding out,
(if only I could have managed it,
to lift it out myself),   740

I attached the two-pronged hoe
to a weak and rotten piece of rope.
It broke on me immediately.

GETAS

That's really good!

SIMICHE

Unhappy me—I've heaved the hoe
into the well with the pail.

GETAS

Now all that's left for you to do
is just to throw yourself in too.

SIMICHE

It just so happens he's getting ready
to move some dung that's lying around.   750
For quite a while he's been searching and shouting,
dashing about and—banging the door!
(Simiche hides by the door as Knemon rushes out.)

GETAS *(to Simiche)*

Get moving—you miserable old woman—
move! He'll kill you. No, protect yourself.

KNEMON

Where's the thief?

SIMICHE *(emerging from her hiding place)*

Master, it fell against my will.

KNEMON

Just start walking inside.

SIMICHE

Tell me, what will you do?

KNEMON
    I'll tie you to the rope and let you down.

SIMICHE
    Please, no. Oh, misery.   760

GETAS
    That's the best use for this same rope—
    by the gods!—if it's totally rotten.

SIMICHE
    I'll call on Daos from the neighbor's house.

KNEMON *(stopping her)*
    You'll call Daos? Damn you,
    you've destroyed me. Go faster—inside!
(Simiche goes into the house.)
    I'm miserable with this emptiness—
    like no other. I'll descend into the well.
    What else is there for me to do?

GETAS *(to Knemon)*
    We'll get a hook and a rope.

KNEMON
    May the gods destroy you utterly   770
    and horribly, if you speak to me.

GETAS
    It would only be right! He's jumped in again.
    What a confounded wretch he is!
    The sort of life he leads! A tried and true
    example of an Attic farmer
    in battle with the rocks that yield
    only thyme and sage. He brings in pain
    but reaps no good from it.
    But here's my master coming

and bringing his guests along.   780
They're just local workers! How odd!
Why now is he leading them here?
How have they become familiar?

SOSTRATOS *(enters, talking to Gorgias and Daos)*
I can't allow you to do otherwise.

GORGIAS
We have all we need.

SOSTRATOS
Heracles! Who could refuse completely
to share a meal with a celebrating friend,
for I am your friend, you should know that's true—
Long before I ever saw you, I was.
Daos, take these things, and then come in.   790

GORGIAS
I can't leave my Mother alone at home.
(to Daos)
Take care of what she needs; I'll be there soon.

ACT IV

(For the second time, Simiche rushes desperately out of Knemon's house in parody of a tragic messenger.)

SIMICHE
Who can rescue us? O wretched me! Who can rescue us?

SIKON *(emerging from the shrine)*
Lord Heracles!
(to Simiche)
Let us get on with our libations
in the name of the gods and divinities.
You are abusive, you beat on us.
Go on with your howling. What a crazy house!

SIMICHE
> My master's in the well.

SIKON
> How's that?   800

SIMICHE
> I'll tell you how—he descended
> to retrieve the hoe and pail,
> when suddenly he slipped on the rim,
> and that's how he fell in.

SIKON
> Not that horrible old man?

SIMICHE
> That's the one.

SIKON
> By heavens, he's done well for himself!
> My dear old woman—now you've got a job to do.

SIMICHE
> But how?

SIKON
> A mortar or stone or something like that—   810
> hurl it at him from above.

SIMICHE *(pleading)*
> Dear man, go down . . .

SIKON
> By Poseidon, I would pay
> if I fight with a dog in the well,
> as the story goes. Never!

SIMICHE *(moving away from him toward Gorgias' house)*
　　Gorgias, where on earth are you?

GORGIAS *(hearing her and coming out of the shrine)*
　　Where am I? What is it, Simiche?

SIMICHE
　　What? I'll say it again.
　　The master's in the well.

GORGIAS *(calling into the shrine)*
　　Sostratos, come out.　　　　　　　　　　　　　　　　820
(to Simiche, as Sostratos comes out of the shrine)
　　You lead the way inside. Go quickly now.
(After the three of them go into Knemon's house, Sikon speaks.)

SIKON
　　There really are gods, by Dionysus!
　　You wouldn't offer a small stew-pot
　　to the worshipers, you sacrilege.
　　You grudge everything. Go fall in the well
　　and drink it down. Then you won't even
　　have water to offer anyone.
(aside)
　　Now the Nymphs have taken revenge
　　on him, as he deserves.
　　No one escapes unharmed, if he harms a cook.　　　830
　　Somehow our art is sacrosanct.
　　You can do what you want to the waiters.
(He hears noises from behind the house.)
　　What's that? He didn't die?
　　A girl is wailing "Dearest Papa."
　　I don't care . . . but it's clear they're hauling him up.
(He imagines the scene.)
　　Just look at him, can you believe it
　　by the gods! Soaked and shivering—elegant!
(pointing to the emblem of Apollo Agyieus by the door)

By this Apollo here, I'd like to see it!
(calling to the women in the shrine)
> You women, pour your libations
> for these rescuers. Pray that they   840
> save the old man—scarcely.
> Let him be maimed and lame—
> no longer will this neighbor be the greatest pain
> to the ever-present worshipers.
> I care how it goes—whenever someone cares to pay.

(Sikon joins his customers in the shrine as Sostratos emerges.)

SOSTRATOS *(to the audience)*
> By Demeter, by Asclepius,
> by the gods, never in my life
> have I witnessed a more opportune
> near-drowning. What a lovely time!
> As fast as we got in, Gorgias jumped down   850
> into the well, while I and the girl
> did nothing from above.
> What could we possibly do?
> Except that she was broken up
> and tore her hair and beat her breast.
> I was precious—just like a nurse,
> by the gods! I stood there and told her
> not to act that way. I begged her,
> looking at her as an image
> of perfect design. The stricken man   860
> was no concern of mine, except
> for all that heaving on the rope.
> What a pain! By Zeus, I nearly destroyed him—
> Looking at my girl, I dropped the rope
> three times. Gorgias was a true Atlas.
> He kept it up and brought him up,
> and when the old man got out, I came here.
> I could hardly keep myself in check.
> I was just THIS close to kissing her.

I love her dreadfully. I'm preparing—   870
oh, they're making noise at the door.
(The door of Knemon's house opens and Knemon emerges, lying on
a wheeled bed like a wounded tragic hero. His
daughter and Gorgias are in attendance. Myrrhine
comes out from the shrine and stands to the side
with her attendants.)

SOSTRATOS *(continuing)*
    O Savior Zeus, how odd!

GORGIAS *(to Knemon)*
    Knemon, tell me what you want.

KNEMON
    What's the use of talking? I feel awful.

GORGIAS
    Bear up!

KNEMON
    I've borne enough. No longer
    will Knemon ever bother you.

GORGIAS
    That's the evil of isolation,
    don't you see? You come within a hair
    of dying recently. Someone should   880
    look after you at your time of life.

KNEMON
    Although I know I'm done for,
    call your mother, Gorgias.

GORGIAS
    Right away.
(aside)
    Troubles alone can teach us,
    as it seems to me.

KNEMON *(without responding to him)*
    Daughter, would you give me your hand
    and help me to stand?

SOSTRATOS *(rushing over, in envy of their close contact; aside)*
    Lucky man!

KNEMON *(to Sostratos)*
    Why are you standing over there,   890
    you miserable specimen?
(to Myrrhine and Gorgias, when Sostratos doesn't answer)
    I wanted hard work, Myrrhine.
    Gorgias, I chose this way of life
    No one could have changed my mind, believe me.
(to all assembled, as an explanation of his life)
    Perhaps I was mistaken, but I thought
    that I alone of everyone
    could be sufficient to myself,
    needing no one else.
    But now I see how fierce and unexpected
    the end of life can be. I've discovered   900
    what I never realized before:
    we must have someone close at hand—
    an ally always ready with assistance.
    But—by Hephaestus—I was so far gone
    from looking at the lives men lead
    and the way they make their calculations
    to profit themselves. I didn't believe
    that anyone could be an altruist.
    That's what got in my way.
    But one man—Gorgias—has proved the reverse,   910
    having done what only the noblest would do.
    I never allowed him to come to my door
    or gave him help of any sort,
    never addressed him, spoke kindly
    but he saved me anyway.

Someone else would have said, and rightly so,
"You never let me come, so I'm not coming now.
You never were of any use,
and that's how I'll reciprocate."
(to Gorgias, personally, noticing his discomfort)
What is it, my boy? If I should die   920
(and I think I will—I'm feeling terrible)
or whether I escape with my life,
in either case, I make you my son.
All that I happen to have, consider your own.
I hand my daughter over to you—
provide her with a husband. If I were well,
I'd never find one on my own—
there isn't anyone who'd please me.
But as for me, if I should live,
allow me to live as I wish,   930
while you take care of all the other things.
You're sensible—with the help of the gods,
you're her proper guardian.
Divide my property and offer half
as dowry for her. Manage the rest
for me and your mother.
(getting tired, to his daughter)
Daughter, help me lie down. I don't believe
a man should speak beyond necessity,
except, my child, I want you to know
a few things about me and my habits.   940
If all the others were like me,
there wouldn't be any law-courts,
and no one would send anyone to jail.
There'd be no war—each man would hold
a moderate share and be content.
If instead, you'd rather follow present paths,
then that's what you should do.
This harsh, dyspeptic aged man won't bother you.

GORGIAS
>All these things I take with thanks,
>but, with your help, as soon as possible,   950
>a husband must be found, if you agree.

KNEMON
>I told you what I thought.
>Now, by the gods, don't bother me.

GORGIAS *(pointing to Sostratos)*
>It just so happens that he wants . . .

KNEMON
>Never, by the gods!

GORGIAS *(continuing)*
>He's someone asking for the girl.

KNEMON
>I don't care about any such things.

GORGIAS
>He helped save you.

KNEMON
>Who's that?

GORGIAS *(bringing Sostratos forward)*
>This man here.   960

KNEMON *(to Sostratos)*
>You, come here.
>*(looks at Sostrates and speaks to Gorgias)*
>He's sunburned. Is he a farmer?

GORGIAS
      He is, father—not one of those
      who puts on airs and ambles lazily around.
      (Knemon nods in agreement, and then has had enough.)

KNEMON
      Wheel me back inside.

GORGIAS *(to Simiche at the door)*
      Take care of him.
      (Knemon goes into his house. Myrrhine and the girl follow.)

SOSTRATOS *(to Gorgias)*
      For the rest, you've got to pledge your sister to me.

GORGIAS
      These things should be referred to your father.

SOSTRATOS
      Father won't say otherwise.

GORGIAS
      Therefore, I certainly give her to you   970
      in view of all the gods. It's fitting, Sostratos
      you've approached this business without disguise
      and honestly. You thought it worth your while
      to work at anything to make this marriage work.
      You're delicate and yet you took up the hoe;
      you dug and wore yourself out.
      In such a manner, a man reveals himself
      when he is prosperous but makes himself
      the equal of a man who's poor.
      With inner strength, your sort will bear   980
      a change of fortune. You've given sufficient proof
      of character. Only remain as you are.

SOSTRATOS *(eagerly)*
    I'll do better yet.
(hesitating)
    And yet to praise
    myself perhaps reveals vulgarity.
(noticing Kallippides coming on stage at the right)
    My father's coming just in time, I see.

GORGIAS *(surprised)*
    Your father is Kallippides?

SOSTRATOS
    Very much indeed!

GORGIAS
    By Zeus, he's rich!

SOSTRATOS
    And rightly so—he's an unbeatable farmer.   990

KALLIPPIDES *(approaching)*
    Looks like I've been left behind. Probably
    they ate up the sheep and returned to the farm.

GORGIAS *(to Sostratos)*
    By Poseidon, he has hunger pains!
    Should we wait or tell him now?

SOSTRATOS
    First let him eat. Later he'll be milder.

KALLIPPIDES *(to Sostratos)*
    What's this Sostratos? Have you eaten?

SOSTRATOS
    Yes, but yours is set aside—go on.

KALLIPPIDES
> I'm on my way in.
> *(He goes into the shrine.)*

GORGIAS
> Go in and talk to him now if you wish—
> just you and your father alone.   1000

SOSTRATOS
> You'll wait in the house, won't you?

GORGIAS
> I'm not coming out.

SOSTRATOS
> I'll leave in a little and call you over.
> *(Sostratos goes into the shrine and Gorgias joins the rest of his family in
>   Knemon's house. When the stage is empty, the
>   Chorus of revelers returns with its paean before the
>   final act.)*

ACT V

> *(When the stage is empty, Kallippides and Sostratos come out of the
> shrine. They are in the middle of a disagreement.)*

SOSTRATOS
> It's not everything I wanted, father.
> I didn't expect this from you.

KALLIPPIDES
> What? Didn't I give way?
> I said that you could have the girl you love.
> I wish it and I say it's got to be.

SOSTRATOS
> That's not how it seems to me.

KALLIPPIDES

> I realize that when you're young,   1010
> marriage turns out to be strong
> when a man is moved by love.

SOSTRATOS

> So I can have this young man's sister
> and consider him worthy of us?
> How can you say he can't have mine?

KALLIPPIDES

> What you say is disgraceful.
> I don't want a beggarly bridegroom and bride.
> One or the other is enough for us.

SOSTRATOS

> You're talking money—an uncertain matter.
> If you knew that it would remain with you   1020
> until the end of time—protect it
> and don't hand it over to a soul.
> But where you lack control, and all you have depends on luck
> > and not on you—
> why should you grudge—O Father!—anyone?
> For Lady Luck could take it all away
> and give your holdings over
> by some mischance to an undeserving man.
> That's why I say, as long as you master it
> you must use it with nobility.
> Be of help to all, and through your actions,   1030
> make as many well-provided as you can.
> Good deeds don't die. Then, if Fortune trips you up,
> these same resources will return to you,
> a visible friend preferable by far
> to secret wealth you've buried in the ground.

KALLIPPIDES

You know how it is, Sostratos—
what I've amassed, I haven't hidden for myself—
How could that be? It's yours.
You've passed your judgment on a man
and want to secure him as a friend?   1040
Why are you giving me maxims?
Go ahead, Sostratos—offer and share.
I'm completely persuaded by you.

SOSTRATOS

You're willing?

KALLIPPIDES

I'm willing, believe me.
Don't bother yourself about it.

SOSTRATOS

Now I'll call Gorgias.
(He calls over toward Knemon's house and Gorgias comes out.)

GORGIAS

I heard you both since I was by the door—
all the things you said from the start.
What then? I consider you my friend,   1050
Sostratos, and I'm extremely fond of you,
but I don't want more than I can manage.
By Zeus, I couldn't do it if I wished.

SOSTRATOS

I don't know what you're saying.

GORGIAS

I give you my sister as your wife,
but to take yours—that would be very fine for me!

SOSTRATOS
    What do you mean by "fine"?

GORGIAS
    It wouldn't be pleasant for me
    to luxuriate in someone else's labors,
    but just in what I've accomplished myself.   1060

SOSTRATOS
    You're talking nonsense, Gorgias.
    How can you judge yourself
    unworthy of this marriage?

GORGIAS
    I've judged myself worthy of her.
    But it isn't right to take a lot
    if you only have a little.

KALLIPPIDES
    By Zeus, how you act the aristocrat!

GORGIAS
    How?

KALLIPPIDES
    By not wishing to appear indulged.
    You've seen me persuaded; it's your turn to yield.   1070
    Your manner convinced me double-fold;
    now don't you be brainless as well as poor.
    Marriage will bring you real security.
(*After a pause, Gorgias agrees.*)

GORGIAS
    You've won. What remains is for us to get engaged.

KALLIPPIDES

> I pledge my daughter now to you
> young man, to produce lawful offspring.
> Three talents as dowry, I offer with her.

GORGIAS

> And I've one talent for my sister.

KALLIPPIDES

> Have you? You shouldn't give too much.

GORGIAS

> But I have it.   1080

KALLIPPIDES

> Keep possession of your total holdings,
> Gorgias. Now bring your mother
> and your sister here to join our women.

GORGIAS

> That's what I should do.

SOSTRATOS

> Let's all stay here and celebrate tonight.
> Tomorrow is the time for marrying.
> Gorgias, bring the old man here.
> His needs will be better cared for by us.

GORGIAS

> He won't want to come, Sostratos.

SOSTRATOS

> Change his mind.   1090

GORGIAS

> If I could.

SOSTRATOS *(to Kallippides)*
>   Father, it's time for a fine round of drinks
>   and an all-night feast for the women.

KALLIPPIDES
>   The reverse, I think—the women will drink
>   while we'll be the ones awake at night.
>   I'll go and get things ready for you.
(Kallippides goes into the shrine.)

SOSTRATOS *(to the audience)*
>   Do it, please.
>   No problem should cause a thinking man
>   To ever fall victim to despair—
>   Application and care can conquer all!   1100
>   I'm the perfect example!
>   In just one day I prevailed,
>   arranging a marriage for myself
>   which no one thought anyone could.
(Gorgias comes out of Knemon's house with his sister and mother.)

GORGIAS *(to the women)*
>   Come forward quickly, will you please.

SOSTRATOS *(to Myrrhine and the girl)*
>   Come this way.
(to his mother at the entrance to the shrine)
>   Mother, receive these women.
(to Gorgias)
>   Knemon hasn't come yet?

GORGIAS
>   He begged me to take the old lady—
>   so he'd be left alone at last.   1110

SOSTRATOS
>   You can't win against him!

GORGIAS

That's the way he is.

SOSTRATOS

But you should enjoy yourself—let's go in.

GORGIAS

Sostratos, I'm embarrassed
to be together with women . . .

SOSTRATOS

Isn't that foolish? Won't you go in?
Now you must take all of us as family.

(Gorgias hesitantly agrees and they go into the shrine together.
Immediately afterward, Simiche comes out of
Knemon's house, talking to Knemon in a mixture
of sympathy and disapproval.)

SIMICHE

I'm going off, by Artemis.
You can just lie there alone.
You make yourself miserable.   1120
They wanted to take you to visit the god,
and you said no. Something bad will happen—
by Demeter and the maiden,
even worse than now. (May all go well!)

(Simiche walks over to the entrance of the shrine, just as Getas is coming
out, telling someone he will check up on Knemon.
At this point, a piper starts to play, and the
following scene is performed with the music in the
background. The atmosphere becomes less realistic
as Knemon is tormented into celebrating with the
others. The music helps create an atmosphere of
fantasy, so that Knemon's miseries at the hands of
Getas and Sikon seem less like cruelty and more
like ritual. Pan will not be denied.)

GETAS *(speaking back into the shrine)*
    I'll go there and see how he is.
(The music begins.)
    Why are you piping for me, you wretch?
    I have no leisure yet.
    I've been sent to the sick man over there
    Hold off a bit!

SIMICHE *(to Getas at the entrance)*
    Let someone else sit with him, inside.   1130
    I want to chat with my lady,
    before she leaves as a bride,
    to talk to her before we're separated.

GETAS
    That's smart of you—now carry on
    I'll see to him while you are gone.
(As Simiche goes into the shrine, Getas calls to Sikon.)
    Hey, Sikon, cook, come over here
    and hear what I have to say—
    I think we'll have some fun today.
(Sikon comes out of the shrine.)
    We'll burn him up—it will be such a pleasure.

SIKON
    What frightens me is Gorgias.   1140
    If he finds out, he'll clean the floor with us.

GETAS
    There's such a lot of noise inside the shrine.
    No one will notice—there's too much wine.
    We'll civilize him into this family
    If he continues as he is,
    We'd all suffer unbearably.

SIKON

There's nothing more that you could say!

GETAS

Only watch out so nobody sees
as you bring him up to the front. Lead the way!

SIKON

I beg you, for a little, wait around—   1150
you can't just disappear from sight—
and, by the gods! don't make a sound.

GETAS

I'm not making noise, by Gaia! Go right!
*(They arrive at Knemon's house and look inside. Then Sikon goes in and
carries Knemon out to the center of the stage.)*

SIKON *(to Getas)*
Look at him!

GETAS

The time is now. That's where to put him.
I'll go first—you watch the rhythm.
(to nonexistent domestic slaves)
Slave, little slave, fine slaves, little slaves!

KNEMON *(waking up)*
Oh my, I'm dying.

GETAS *(calling louder)*
Fine slaves, O slave, little slave, slave, slaves!

KNEMON *(in greater agony this time)*
Oh my, I'm dying.   1160

GETAS

Hello! Who's this fellow? Is this where you live?

KNEMON
No doubt about it. What do you want?

GETAS
Giant bowls and casseroles.

KNEMON
Who can help me to stand?

GETAS
You have them, you truly have all at hand—
seven stools and twelve tables belong to you—
slaves, pass the word to the inside crew.
I'm in a hurry too.

KNEMON
There isn't any.

GETAS *(incredulously)*
There isn't?   1170

KNEMON *(angry)*
Haven't you heard me ten thousand times?

GETAS
I'll make my escape.
(He runs to the side and motions to Sikon to take over.)

KNEMON *(aside)*
Oh, misery! How did I get to be
brought to this spot? Who put me
down in front of my house?

SIKON *(to Getas)*
You go off, I'm on.
Slave, little slave, O women, men, doorman!

KNEMON

> My man, are you mad? You'll bring down the door.

SIKON

> Could you supply nine coverlets?

KNEMON

> How could I?   1180

SIKON

> . . . and a woven Oriental hanging,
> in length, one hundred feet.

KNEMON

> A strap! If only I could beat . . .
> Old woman! Where's the old woman?
> at the sacrifice. You've got to bear
> these indignities—no one's here to help.
> Bite your lip and listen
> to one thing after another:
> when your women came to the cave,
> hugs and handshakes greeted your wife   1190
> and daughter. Their manner of life
> was not unappealing. I was near
> preparing the entertainment for the men.
> Don't you hear me? Don't go to sleep.

GETAS

> No indeed!

KNEMON

> Oh me!

SIKON

> What then? You don't want to be there?
> We were hurrying—here's what follows—

I readied the table and spread the pillows—
do you hear? The cushions and tables were set—   1200
I just happen to be a cook, don't forget.

GETAS *(aside)*
    He's such a dainty fellow!

SIKON *(continuing)*
    Somebody tilted the old Bacchic wine
    into a deep bellied cup.
    With Naiad springs he mixed it up
    And toasted the men in a round.
    Another saluted the women in line:
    They drank it up like sandy ground . . .
    You understand?
    A serving girl was turning tipsy,   1210
    and shaded the flush on her blushing young face.
    She started to pace in a rhythmic trance,
    but hesitating, modestly.
    Another maiden took her hand
    and joined her in the dance.

GETAS *(jumping up to dance and grabbing Knemon)*
    Oh, you've suffered frightfully,
    so dance now, join the chorus.

KNEMON
    What do you wretches want with me?

GETAS
    You country boor, come and dance with us.

KNEMON
    Stop, by the gods!   1220

GETAS
    Then let us bring you in.

KNEMON
> What can I do?

GETAS *(starting to force him to dance again)*
> Then it's dancing for you!

KNEMON
> Take me in—better there than here.

GETAS
> Now you're talking sensibly.
> We win! O lovely victory!
> Slave, O Donax, Sikon, Syrus!
> Bring him in along with us.

(Donax and Syrus, two slaves without speaking parts, pick Knemon up
from the ground and start to carry him into the
shrine. Before they go in, Getas speaks.)

GETAS *(to Knemon)*
> Just watch yourself, 'cause if we catch
> you giving trouble again, we won't react so moderately—   1230
> We'll really deal with you then!
(to the servants)
> Someone bring us garlands and a torch.

SIKON *(to Getas, handing him a garland from the altar of Apollo)*
> Take this one here.

(Sikon, Syrus, and Donax bring Knemon into the shrine as Getas speaks
the epilogue to the audience.)

GETAS
> Proceed. Now you've seen us triumphant
> over this troublesome old man.
> Your warm applause now, if you please,
> dear lads and boys and men. May laughter-loving Victory,
> noble-born and maidenly, favor us forever.

Desperately Seeking Justice (Epitrepontes)

Translated by
Sheila D'Atri and Palmer Bovie

Translators' Preface

The *Epitrepontes*, here *Desperately Seeking Justice*, is an abandoned baby story. Like the infant Moses, like the heroes in classical melodramas, the baby is returned to his rightful parents in the end. The comic twists make this play unique. Literally, *Epitrepontes* means "men going about an arbitration." In the central scene of the play the exposed child, found by a shepherd and given over to a charcoal-burner, becomes the object of a dispute when the two men argue over the jewelry and other items that were left with the child. Ironically, it is the unknown grandfather, who just happens to be passing by, whom they choose to decide between them and determine the fate of the baby.

The drama opens in the countryside, somewhere between Athens and a village where a festival named the Tauropolia was held. It was celebrated with music and dancing in honor of Artemis Tauropolos during all-night revels for women. It was at this festival the year before that the baby was conceived during a drunken attack on the innocent Pamphile, the daughter of Smikrines (a common name in comedy, often indicating one given to small-mindedness, but in this play a stodgy but upright gentleman).

A twofold problem needs to be solved—the baby's mother and father must both be found. By a twist of fate, they are now unhappily married to each other. Charisios, the husband, has put aside all memory of his inebriated assault on a girl in the dark, but is harboring bitter feelings toward his wife since learning from a servant that in his absence she and her old nurse exposed a baby just five months after the wedding. He feels betrayed, and tries to find solace in wine parties and with Habrotonon, a harp-girl he hired as musician and hetaira (courtesan). Pamphile is wretchedly neglected while her father complains bitterly about the wasteful expenses of his son-in-law and wants to take back his daughter and her dowry. The couple love each other, really. Pamphile does not want to leave Charisios and Charisios is a total disappointment as a lover to Habrotonon, using her as a poor distraction from his miseries over Pamphile's supposed betrayal.

Large portions of the beginning of this play are missing, but a prologue deity must have come on stage early in the action to explain the complications of the past and so make the characters and their motivations easier to follow. A reasonable semblance of such a divine prologue has therefore been interpolated into this adaptation of the play, which contains one of Menander's most complicated plots.

How to sort out the mess? First of all, the baby was awarded to a poor and honest couple, Syros, the charcoal-burner and slave of Chairestratos (friend and neighbor to Charisios), and his wife, who has just lost a child. When Onesimos (slave of Charisios) sees the couple looking through the items found with the baby, he recognizes his master's ring and demands its return. Onesimos realizes what the implications are—the ring may very well indicate paternity, and he has already heaped trouble on his head by blabbering about Pamphile's baby (of course not realizing that they are one and the same). However, he could equally be in trouble if he let his master's baby be brought up as a slave. Habrotonon now comes to the rescue. It happens that she was playing the harp for a group of women at the Tauropolia the year before and saw a young girl wander off by herself and come back later crying, with her dress badly torn. She pays close attention to Onesimos when he tells her that his master lost the ring when drunk at the Tauropolia. She tells him that she saw something similar and could question the ladies she played for and so try to find the mother of the baby. She also says that she would recognize the girl if she should see her again.

The father, the mother, the ring, and the baby all need to be connected together. Habrotonon comes up with a clever plan—to be sure that the ring was not given to another culprit as a gambling debt or lost in some way, she decides to go inside wearing the ring herself, pretending that she was the girl at the festival. Charisios' behavior will give him away. After this, Habrotonon, carrying the baby, recognizes Pamphile outside her house and gently questions her about that fatal night. Pamphile is bewildered, thinking it is Habrotonon's child, but Habrotonon tells her that she has just been posing to gain time to find the real mother. Pamphile then asks, "Who's the father?" and is told that it is her own Charisios.

The rest of the play is dedicated to resolutions and a great deal of soul-searching on the part of Charisios after he learns how he became a father. Through his servant Onesimos, we see him hysterically berate himself for showing no mercy to his wife or to the girl he assaulted. He faults himself, tears himself apart, and praises the nobility of his wife who suffered similarly. It is only after some time that he is told by Habrotonon that the child is Pamphile's as well. Joyous, his shattered self-image restored by his wife's forgiveness, he and Pamphile can begin their marriage again in full reconciliation. A celebration is in order for the dramatis personae and a victory prayer for the author.

Cast

KARION, a cook
ONESIMOS, slave of Charisios
PEITHO, goddess of Persuasion
SMIKRINES, father of Pamphile
CHAIRESTRATOS, friend and neighbor of Charisios
HABROTONON, harp-girl and hetaira hired by Charisios
CHORUS of young revelers
SYROS, charcoal-burner (slave of Chairestratos)
DAOS, shepherd
PAMPHILE, wife of Charisios
CHARISIOS, young man of Attica
NONSPEAKING
   Baby
   Sophrone, old nurse of Pamphile, slave of Smikrines
   Wife of Syros
   Simias, Karion's assistant

(A village street near Athens. Two houses are seen on stage, one
belonging to Charisios and the other to Chairestratos.)

   ACT I

(Karion, the inquisitive cook, and Onesimos, the busybody slave of
   Charisios, are intensely involved in their gossip about the recent
   affairs of Charisios.)

KARION
   Hasn't your master, Onesimos,
   taken the harp-girl Habrotonon
   to live with as his mistress?
   By the gods, now, isn't it true
   that he's only recently married?

ONESIMOS
That really is what's happened.

KARION
I like that about you, you're ready to talk.
You also like to know what's happening
behind the scenes. I think there's nothing sweeter
than being wholly in the know.   10

ONESIMOS
There are limits, Karion.
My master seems to be messing around
in the house of his friend, while his wife
is waiting and moping at home.
She always looked like an innocent girl,
but five months after the wedding,
while Charisios was traveling,
a baby was born, abandoned by her
and Sophrone. It's in the countryside
somewhere, and when my master came back home,   20
I thought it right to tell him so—
and so he went to live next door.
Sometimes I wish I hadn't said a word,
and I wish even more for a happier home.
(Onesimos pauses in his reflections and speaks sharply to the cook.)
Go and do your job and get his dinner.
He's been lying about and fretting forever.
All you are doing is standing around
looking for all the world like a jug
with a huge and gaping mouth.
And as for me, by gabbing here with you—   30
I may have added salt to salted fish,
if this should turn out even worse.

KARION *(exiting to the right, toward town)*
Trust me. Soon I'll be back with the rest of the food.

ONESIMOS

    I'd try to help my master, but I fear
    that if I meddle and then make a mess,
    the blows will fall on me.

(Onesimos also departs into Chairestratos' house. The stage is empty for
               a moment; then the goddess Peitho, Persuasion,
               appears to explain the situation to the audience.)

PEITHO

    We have a complicated situation here.
    Charisios is in love with Pamphile,
    the wife he thinks has cheated him.
    He suffers and tries to soothe his sadness   40
    with wine and the harp-girl he hired
    (although in truth he takes no pleasure there,
    and faithfully stays angry with his wife).
    He blames her, feels betrayed, and yet the guilty
    man is (unknown to himself) himself.
    He was the brute who caused their misery.
    The girl was raped, attacked, in shock.
    Innocent and helpless in the dark,
    she could not recognize the man (her groom to be)
    who, drunk and wild, assaulted her   50
    at the Tauropolia, a women's festival.
    This will all be known, but first our characters
    must establish with great care and kindness
    (and help from me), the parentage
    of this poor foundling child. So far he's safe,
    rescued by a humble charcoal vendor,
    a servant of our friend Chairestratos.
    Trouble will arise, but I'll be sure
    this baby keeps the ring and things he needs
    to prove his free birth and identity.   60

(pauses and looks off stage)

    Now I see the "grandpa" coming in from town.
    He has a role to play in this, although

he has no clue to what is going on.
He's hurting for his daughter while his stingy soul
is fuming at his wasteful son-in-law.
Since he's approaching, I must now be off.
(Peitho leaves stage as Smikrines enters, muttering furiously.)

SMIKRINES
A lazy man who's healthy is much worse
than one who's sick. The healthy one eats double,
but it's all for nothing. Take my son-in-law
(please—do take him!)   70
he not only eats a dowry up,
he also drinks it down with wine,
and wine that isn't cheap by any means.
It's not that he's drunk that I'm complaining about—
what I find unbelievable
is that he'll spend a five on half a bottle
and drink it up all by himself.
*(Chairestratos comes out of his house and sees Smikrines. He speaks in
an aside to the audience.)*

CHAIRESTRATOS
I expected this. He'll push his way
into my house and mess up our cozy affair.
But why should I care? I told him before   80
to go and hang himself, and here he is.

SMIKRINES *(ignoring Chairestratos)*
He's taken four talents from me as a dowry,
and yet he doesn't think to share a home
with his own wife. He sleeps apart from her
and pays some whorehouse-keeper
twelve drachmas every day.

CHAIRESTRATOS
At least he's got that right. Where cost's concerned
he knows his business.

SMIKRINES *(continuing to himself)*
>That's enough to feed a man for a month,
>and probably for six days more.   90

CHAIRESTRATOS
>He's good at counting. Two obols a day
>is enough for barley when you're starving—
>or maybe once upon a time it was.
(Habrotonon comes out of Chairestratos' house and speaks to him.)

HABROTONON
>Chairestratos—Charisios is waiting—
>Sweetie, who's that standing over there?

CHAIRESTRATOS
>It's the father of *his wife.*

HABROTONON
>He looks like a philosopher,
>three times full of gloom and doom.

SMIKRINES *(addressing Habrotonon and Chairestratos)*
>So *you're* the harp-girl, and *you're* providing the house
>for Charisios to entertain   100
>while Pamphile his wife waits all alone.
>I want my daughter and my dowry back,
(to Habrotonon)
>Why don't you go back and grub after gold
>from some fool who hasn't a wife to support?

HABROTONON *(to Smikrines, looking offended)*
>Don't speak to me in that insulting way.
>Do you think it will do you any good?

SMIKRINES
>Go perch with the crows, and screech with them too.
>You'll suffer for this. I'm going inside,

I want to know how my daughter is doing,
in every detail. Then I'll go after him—   110
that wastrel, her husband—however I can.
(Smikrines goes into Charisios' house to speak with his daughter
                        Pamphile. Habrotonon and Chairestratos are alone
                        on stage.)

HABROTONON
    Shall we go and tell Charisios who's come?

CHAIRESTRATOS
    We should warn him. What a cunning fox
    that old man is. He makes a house
    turn upside down.

HABROTONON *(joking)*
    I'd like many houses just like that!
    (It's good for my profession.)

CHAIRESTRATOS
    Many?

HABROTONON
    Certainly I like the one next door.
(aside)
    That's the one where I find *you*.   120

CHAIRESTRATOS
    You mean *my* house?

HABROTONON
    Yes, yours. We should join Charisios.

CHAIRESTRATOS
    Let's go now, for I see a gang
    of teen-aged drunks coming right this way.
    It's not the best time to bump into them!
(Chorus of young revelers appears for the entr'acte performance.)

CHORUS
>At the drinking-party we made our vows
>(and covered the altar with flowers)
>to avoid all drunken violence
>and dampen our pride in our powers.
>Did we promise to tell only reverent tales   130
>when the wine was still in the kraters?
>We filled our cups and we're stewed to the gills—
>now we're ready to play-act as satyrs.

>### ACT II
>*(Onesimos comes out of Chairestratos' house, looking for Karion.)*

ONESIMOS *(annoyed)*
>That cook comes around to hear gossip
>but he's gone when you need him to work.

(reflectively)
>I never was the sort to suppose
>that human situations are all safe.
>There's always risk in the mix of things,
>and now I'm sorry I told him the story
>about what happened with the baby.   140
>It's Pamphile he loves, I'm sure of that,
>but now that old miser, her father
>wants a return of his daughter and dowry.
>My master cares and doesn't seem to care,
>and something's wrong that I don't understand.

(pauses and looks down the street)
>That cook can certainly jaw on the job.
>I must be sure that all is provided
>for those endless parties, day and night,
>but my master's morose and hard to please
>and has no taste for food. He only wants   150
>to serve his guests, but for himself he seeks
>diversion and oblivion in wine,
>pretends a passing interest in the harp-girl,
>but moves away whenever she comes near to him.

(looks toward Charisios' house)

Pamphile's father's coming outside now.
Anything he does will make things worse.
(*Smikrines approaches Onesimos and speaks to him.*)

SMIKRINES (*in angry frustration*)
I'm sure you've somehow had a hand in this.
My daughter's wretched husband guzzles up
her portion, and you're the one who helps him.
As for her, I cannot understand   160
why she insists on staying as his wife.
She is and yet she isn't, and she won't
listen to reason when it comes from me.
You should tell your master that divorce
is the only decision that makes sense.
Perhaps your saying it will make things clear.

ONESIMOS
I'm just his slave, I have no power
to persuade, but if I have the chance
to help your daughter, sir, I will.
(*Onesimos goes back into Chairestratos' house. For a few moments
            Smikrines is alone on stage. Then, from the
            countryside on the left, enter the charcoal-burner
            Syros, a slave of Chairestratos, accompanied by
            his wife and a baby, and the shepherd Daos. They
            are in the middle of an argument as they slowly
            approach Smikrines, who at first barely notices
            them.*)

SYROS (*to Daos*)
You're on the defense and you know it,   170
trying to get away with something wrong.

DAOS (*angrily*)
You miserable toad, you have no right
to take possession of what isn't yours.

SYROS

    An arbitrator must be found
    to settle this fight about these ornaments.

DAOS

    Let's find a judge, I want one too.

SYROS

    Who, then, shall we get who will decide?

DAOS

    All the same to me. I want what's rightly mine.
    Oh, why did I offer anything to you?

SYROS *(by now standing next to Smikrines and nodding toward him)*
    Are you willing to take that man as our judge?   180

DAOS

    I think it's good luck to find someone now.

SYROS *(speaking to Smikrines)*
    By the gods, sir, might you have a bit of leisure
    and give us a little of your time?

SMIKRINES *(startled out of his thoughts, testily)*
    To you? About what?

SYROS *(very politely)*
    There's a dispute between us about a matter . . .

SMIKRINES

    Why does that matter to me?

SYROS

    We're looking for a judge without a bias.
    If nothing prevents you, settle it for us.

SMIKRINES *(annoyed)*
You lousy looking losers, do you go around
disputing cases, wearing leather jerkins?   190

SYROS *(still polite and humble)*
Nevertheless, the matter is brief
and easy to learn the terms of it all.
Make it a favor, don't look down on us.
In everything, in every way, justice
that is timely is everyone's concern.
It's a problem that's common in life.

DAOS *(looking restless and aggrieved)*
I've batted heads with quite an orator.
Oh, why did I ever offer to share?

SMIKRINES *(relenting)*
Tell me, will it stand, whatever I shall judge?

SYROS
Completely.   200

SMIKRINES
I will hear you out. Why, what prevents me?
You, over there, the quiet one, speak first.

DAOS
I must go back a bit, it's not only
about what happened between me and him,
so that should make the matters clear to you.
In the thicket near this area,
I've shepherded my sheep some thirty days,
by myself, alone, good sir, and then one day
I found a child, a baby, lying there
wearing a necklace and some ornaments.   210

SYROS *(breaking in, excitedly)*
> And *those ornaments* are the problem!

DAOS *(protesting)*
> He doesn't let me speak.

SMIKRINES *(lifting his walking-stick, pointing it at Syros)*
> If you babble in between his words
> I'll settle this stick upon you.

SYROS *(humbly)*
> And with justice too.

SMIKRINES *(to Daos)*
> Now speak.

DAOS
> I continue my speech. I picked it up
> and went back home, bringing it, thinking
> that I would raise the child myself.
> The idea seemed good to me then,   220
> when I hadn't the time to think it out.
> And then, at night, I reasoned with myself
> as all men do, giving more thought to it all,
> and I thought "Why should I bear the troubles
> of bringing up a child? What about the
> expenditure and all his other needs?
> Why should I have all those worries?"
> Well, that's the way I was. And then, at dawn
> I went back to my sheep, and then *he* came—
> he's a man who burns charcoal—to that same place   230
> to burn some stumps. We'd met and spoken
> many times before. We talked together,
> since he saw me looking worried. "Daos,
> what's on your mind?" he said, and then I said

"I've been a busy-body," and told him
how I found the child and how I picked it up.
Then right away, before I even finished,
he kept saying "Daos, please" and "bless you"
after every single phrase while he kept saying
"give me the child, and this will bring you luck   240
and may you be forever free" and that's how he
was pleading. He said "I have a wife
and our baby died when she was giving birth."
He was talking about this woman here,
the one who's holding the infant.

SMIKRINES *(to Syros)*
    And were you asking like that?

DAOS *(bursting in)*
    He wore me down the whole day long
    with his begging. I couldn't hold out
    against his perseverance and his promises.
    And so I gave him the child and he went off,   250
    raining a thousand blessings upon me.
    He even bent down and kissed my hands.

SMIKRINES *(to Syros)*
    Did you do all that?

SYROS
    I admit that I did.

DAOS
    He'd made his escape and now I find him back,
    coming around with his wife to me now
    and suddenly he wants those things that once
    were left behind with the baby. Small things,
    frivolous, bits of nothing, but he says
    I'm treating him badly since I refuse   260
    to hand everything over to him.

I say he should be grateful for the share
he got by all his pleading. There was no need
for me to give him everything. "Hermes shared"—
that's what we say—since windfalls go to all.
If we'd been walking together, then the find
would go half to me and half to him—
But I was alone and found them alone
and he wasn't there. So how can he stand here
and say it all belongs to him, while nothing   270
goes to me.

(to Syros)
           I gave you one of my things—
if it still pleases you, then keep it
and if it doesn't, give it back to me.
Just don't change your mind and then come back
to say you were cheated. You should not have it all—
one part given willingly, the other forced from me.
Now I have finished speaking my speech.

SYROS *(slightly sarcastic, to Smikrines)*
Has he really finished?

SMIKRINES
Didn't you hear? He has spoken.

SYROS
Very well. Now I will speak on what comes after.   280
He did find this child by himself, and all
those things he's said are right—it happened that way sir,
and I won't speak against it. Begging and pleading,
I took the child from him—he tells the truth.
But a shepherd he works with and talked to
let me know he found some jewels with the child.
This child is here and they belong to him.
(He turns to his wife and asks for the baby, which he takes in his arms.)
Give me the baby, my wife.
This child asks you, Daos, for the necklace

and whatever else may prove to be the key   290
to his identity. *He* says they were put there
for *him* and not for your enrichment.
I make this claim since I'm his guardian—
you made me that when you gave him to me.
(to Smikrines)
Now, sir, the judgment is yours, and it turns
upon these adornments, whether they're gold
or made of worthless stuff, and whether this gift
from his mother, whoever she may be,
should be guarded for him till he's grown
and not disappear with this plunderer   300
because he was first to find what wasn't his.
Well then, you may wonder, why I didn't ask
to take them when I took the baby.
I hadn't yet thought of it then—but now
I come on his behalf and not my own—
I ask for nothing for myself.
(to Daos)
                            You said
"Hermes shared" and so should we all share,
but not when that means doing someone wrong.
This isn't a matter of finding—it's stealing.
Look at it this way sir—perhaps this child   310
raised with hard-working slaves, well someday he
may look on us as alien to his nature.
Perhaps his birth is free and he is meant
to hunt down lions, be an officer
or run in the Olympics. You have seen
those tragedies by men like Sophocles
and other famous authors who wrote plays
about the situation we have here.
Think of Neleus and Pelias—they were found
by some old herdsman on a mountain-side   320
abandoned by the princess Tyro,
although their father was Poseidon.
That herdsman wore a leather vest like mine,

but when he saw that they were upper-class,
he told them his story, how he found them
and gave the boys a knapsack full of items
that helped them trace their birth. For when they learned
their history, instead of shepherds, they were kings.
If Daos, though, had taken those items
to make a profit of twelve drachmas,   330
till the end of time those boys would never
know their ancestry. It isn't right
that I should raise the body of this child
while Daos swipes all hope of freedom, sir.
In another story, a man almost married
his sister, but through such tokens of his birth
he was prevented. Another man found his mother
and saved her, while yet another rescued his brother.
We know these stories by Euripides—
Iphigenia, Ion, and Antiope.   340
Life isn't safe, sir, and we must think ahead,
looking ahead to what is possible.
But "Give it back," he says "if you don't like it"
and thinks that this adds power to his case.
That's no longer just.
(to Daos)
                If you must return
one of his things, next time will you seek
to keep the child to hide your thieving?
But now the Goddess Chance has made him safe.
I have spoken.
(to Smikrines)
                Make a judgment that is just.

SMIKRINES
    This arbitration is easy. My judgment is—   350
what was left with the baby is his.

DAOS
    Fine. And what about the child?

SMIKRINES
> By Zeus, I won't decide it's yours—
> you tried to cheat him, but the other man
> helped him and stopped what you attempted.

SYROS *(to Smikrines)*
> May all good things be yours!

DAOS
> This judgment is dreadful, by Zeus the Savior!
> I found it all, I lost it all.
> He found nothing, yet he gets it all.
> *(pauses)*
> Do I have to give everything back?   360

SMIKRINES
> That's what I said.

DAOS
> It's a dreadful judgment, damn it!

SYROS *(asking for the objects)*
> Give it over quickly now.

DAOS *(grumbling)*
> O Heracles, what I have suffered.

SYROS
> Show me the pouch right now. That's where they are.
> *(to Smikrines)*
> I beg you sir, don't go away,
> be sure he'll really give them back.

DAOS *(grumbling)*
> Oh, why did I ever agree to turn to *him*?

SMIKRINES
> Give it over, you criminal.

DAOS *(still balking, but handing them over)*
> I've been treated shamefully!   370

SMIKRINES *(to Syros)*
> Do you have it all now?

SYROS
> I believe I do, that is unless
> he swallowed something while I was speaking
> and he thought he was going to lose.

DAOS
> I don't believe this.

SYROS
> Good luck, sir. All others should mete out justice
> as swiftly and as well as you.
> *(Smikrines goes off on the right side of the stage, which leads to the city.)*

DAOS
> A damnable business. O Heracles,
> no arbitration's been more terrible.

SYROS
> You were rotten.   380

DAOS
> Rotten yourself, and you make sure
> to guard them for *him*, until he's grown.
> Look out, I'll be watching you all the time!
> *(Daos leaves the stage at the left, leading to the country. Syros calls to
> him as he goes.)*

SYROS
Get to hell out of here and go.
(to his wife)
Now take this to our master who lives here
and bring it to Chairestratos himself.
We'll remain in this place now. In the morning,
after we've paid our portion to him,
then we'll start off for work again, my wife.
But first let's count these objects, one by one.   390
Do you have some sort of box? You don't?
Well, then place them in the fold of your robe.

ONESIMOS *(coming out of Chairestratos' house, not aware of the others at
              first)*
No one's ever seen a slower cook.
Why, yesterday, about this time
they were on the after-dinner wine.

SYROS *(talking to his wife)*
This picture looks like a rooster—
a very skinny one at that. Take it.
That one's covered with gems. This is an axe.

ONESIMOS *(approaching them, to Syros)*
What is this all about?

SYROS
This is a ring that's gold on the surface,   400
but iron underneath. Here's a carving
of a bull or a goat—I can't tell which.
Someone named Cleostratos has made it.
That's how the letters around it read.

ONESIMOS *(looking agitated)*
Show it to me now.

SYROS
>Here it is. And who are you?

ONESIMOS *(grabbing the ring and staring at it)*
>This is the one, the very one!

SYROS
>What do you mean? What one?

ONESIMOS
>The ring!

SYROS
>What ring? I cannot understand you.   410

ONESIMOS
>The one my master, Charisios, had.

SYROS
>You're out of your mind.

ONESIMOS
>It's the very ring he lost.

SYROS *(getting angry, putting out his hand)*
>Put that ring back here, you thief!

ONESIMOS
>I should give you what belongs to *us*?
>When did you take it? How did you get it?

SYROS *(weary)*
>By Apollo and the gods, what misery
>to keep things safe for this poor orphan child!
>Someone comes and looks and soon enough

he wants to snatch the objects away.   420
I told you, give me back that ring!

ONESIMOS *(insistent)*
    You're playing around with me.
    It's my master's, by Apollo and the gods!

SYROS *(to his wife)*
    I'd rather have my throat cut open
    before I yield to him. I'll be the judge
    for everyone, and one thing at a time.
    It belongs to the baby, not to me.
    Here's a metal chain-link necklace. Take it.
    Also this folded piece of purple cloth.
    Now bring it all inside.   430
(She goes into Chairestratos' house. Syros turns to Onesimos.)
    Now you, what are you trying to tell me?

ONESIMOS
    Me? Its owner is Charisios.
    He lost it one day when he was drunk.
    Anyway, that's what he told me.

SYROS
    I'm a servant of Chairestratos.
    Keep it safe or give it back to me,
    so I can show it for you to your master.

ONESIMOS
    I'd rather guard it myself.

SYROS
    No difference to me. We're both going
    into this same house here, as it seems.   440

ONESIMOS

> Now they are busy with friends and the time
> may not be right to make disclosures.
> Tomorrow, then.

SYROS

> I'll wait. Tomorrow choose whomever you wish
> to judge this case. In one word—I am ready.

(Onesimos goes into Chairestratos' house with the ring.)

SYROS *(to the audience)*

> Well, I didn't do badly there either.
> I think that my concern and my true business now
> is in dispensing justice. This is the way
> that all things are made safe for us today.

(Syros goes into Chairestratos' house. Chorus of young men returns.)

CHORUS

> Wine is loyal to its friends—   450
> revere the gods and keep the tables clean.
> If you can't remember,
> you can't make amends,
> so in December
> when the moon is lean
> let the torches stay ablaze
> and pray your way home through the haze.

ACT III

> *(Chorus leaves the stage and Onesimos comes out of Chairestratos'*
> *house.)*

ONESIMOS

> As for the ring, on more than five occasions
> I started approaching my master
> to show it to him, but just as soon   460

as I came near him, I delayed.
I regret what I told him before—
for now he often says, "may Zeus destroy
that damned-blasted blabberer who told me
news I didn't want to hear." Now what if
a reconciliation should occur
between him and his wife? He might make me
and my mouth disappear from this world.
I know too much already. Better not
stir up the pot with something else   470
and give myself more trouble than before.

(Habrotonon comes out of Chairestratos' house, speaking to people
inside.)

HABROTONON
Let me go, I beg you, give me no more
problems—I've done enough to myself.
Ignorant and stupid as it seems,
I've already made myself into a joke.
I thought he'd love me, but that man
harbors a weird kind of hate for me now.
He won't allow me to lie on the couch
to eat and drink beside him anymore,
but I must stay dejected and away.   480

ONESIMOS *(looking at the ring, paying no attention to Habrotonon)*
Do I really have to give this back
to the fellow I just took it from? Absurd!

HABROTONON *(considering her own problems, ignoring Onesimos)*
He's wretched too, and also why is he
throwing away so much money on parties?
In my relationship to him, I qualify
to bear a holy basket to Athena,
with the virgin girls. For three days now
already, I've remained chaste by his side.

ONESIMOS *(still absorbed by the ring)*
> How, by the gods, I'm praying, how . . .

(Syros comes out of Chairestratos' house, looks around, then spots
Onesimos.)

SYROS
> Where is he, that fellow I'm following   490
> everywhere inside? Oh, there he is—
> Hey you—give me back the ring, or show it
> as you said you intended. We must have
> a judgment soon, for soon I have to go.

ONESIMOS
> This is the way it is—it's my master's—
> Charisios'—I'm sure. But I shrink
> from showing it to him, for fear that it will show
> that he's the father of that child who wore it.

SYROS *(puzzled)*
> How can that be?

ONESIMOS
> You imbecile—He lost it at the Tauropolia—   500
> an all-night festival for women.
> It stands to reason that a girl was raped
> and bore this child and then had it exposed.
> First find the girl and show the ring to her,
> then the evidence is clear. Now all we have
> is suspicion and confusion.

SYROS
> You yourself should stage a search for the girl.
> But if you want to shake me down and take the ring
> from me, or think I'd give you a little something
> for it, you're a fool. It's not my way to share.   510

ONESIMOS
I don't want that either.

SYROS
All right for now—I'm going into town,
but soon I'll be back, and I'll know what to do.
(Syros exits to the right, toward the city. Habrotonon, who has been
listening, approaches Onesimos.)

HABROTONON
The child the woman is nursing inside,
Onesimos—did the charcoal-burner find it?

ONESIMOS
That's what he says.

HABROTONON
So pretty, that poor little baby.

ONESIMOS *(showing the ring to her)*
And also he said he found with it
this ring belonging to my master.

HABROTONON
Poor child. But if it's really your master's,   520
could you bear to see it brought up as a slave?
You would deserve to die for that.

ONESIMOS
But, as I was saying, nobody knows
whoever the mother might be.

HABROTONON
You say he lost it at the Tauropolia?

ONESIMOS
He was drinking. That's what the slave boy
who went with him said.

HABROTONON

It seems clear he stumbled on the women
at the festival. Something like that happened
as well to a girl in the place where I was.   530

ONESIMOS

You were there?

HABROTONON

Yes, at the Tauropolia last year.
I was playing the lute for some girls,
and I myself played games with them.
I didn't yet know how men could behave.

ONESIMOS

Oh, sure!

HABROTONON

By Aphrodite, I swear it's true.

ONESIMOS

Did you know what girl it was?

HABROTONON

I could ask. She was a friend
of the women I played for.   540

ONESIMOS

Did you hear the name of her father?

HABROTONON

I don't know anything—but if I saw her
I'd know her. She was lovely, by the gods—
and also they said she was wealthy.

ONESIMOS

She could be the one we're looking for.

HABROTONON

> I have no idea. She wandered off from us
> after some time had passed, then suddenly
> she ran up to us crying, all alone,
> pulling out her hair, and by the gods, her gown
> so light and lovely, was destroyed.   550
> It was nothing but a rag.

ONESIMOS

> And did she have this ring with her?

HABROTONON

> It's possible, but if she did,
> she didn't show a thing to me.
> I will not tell a lie.

ONESIMOS

> Well, what should I do now?

HABROTONON

> See to that yourself. But if you have sense,
> take my advice and make everything clear
> to your master. If the child is of free birth,
> then should this fact be hidden away?   560

ONESIMOS *(hesitating)*

> First, let's find out who she is.
> Habrotonon, be my ally in this.

HABROTONON

> I can't—until I know the attacker's name.
> I'm afraid of telling tales to those ladies
> in vain. Maybe someone took it as a pledge
> and lost it. Maybe as a gambling debt,
> or under pressure about some matter
> he gave it up. A thousand other things
> can happen at those drinking-parties.
> Before we find her attacker, I don't want   570

to make an inquiry about the girl
or spread any rumors about her.

ONESIMOS

That's not bad reasoning—so what should be done?

HABROTONON

What do you think about this, Onesimos?
I'll pretend this business pertains to me.
I'll take this ring and go inside to him.

ONESIMOS *(puzzled)*

Repeat what you said—I almost understand.

HABROTONON

He'll see me wearing it and soon he'll ask
how I came to have it. Then I'll answer,
"At the Tauropolia, when I was   580
a virgin girl," and pretend what happened
to her happened to me. Most of it I know.

ONESIMOS

That beats them all!

HABROTONON

If it hits close to home, he will confess
fast and furious, before I say much more,
especially since he's been drinking.
Whatever he says, I will agree with him
and avoid the mistake of saying something first.

ONESIMOS

That tops them all, by the Sun!

HABROTONON

I'll flatter him with common sayings,   590
"You were so strong and reckless," I will say,
careful to make no mistakes.

ONESIMOS
      That's good.

HABROTONON
      I'll add, "You threw me down with so much force
      that my poor dress was utterly destroyed."
      Before that, in the house, I'll take the child
      and cry and show affection, then I'll ask
      the woman where she got it from.

ONESIMOS
      Heracles!

HABROTONON
      Finally I'll say, "It seems you have a baby,"   600
      and then I'll show the ring that's just been found.

ONESIMOS
      Sneaky and devilish, Habrotonon!

HABROTONON
      Then, if we've established he's the father,
      at leisure, we can find the girl.

ONESIMOS
      There's one more thing you didn't say,
      and that's that you'll be free. If he should think
      that you're the mother of his child, at once
      he'll buy your freedom, that is clear.

HABROTONON
      I don't know—but I really would like that!

ONESIMOS
      You don't know? And what about me, Habrotonon—   610
      will anything good come my way from this?

HABROTONON

By the goddesses, you'd be the cause
of all my happiness—I won't forget you.

ONESIMOS

Suppose you decide to stop looking for her,
cheating me, well, what will happen then?

HABROTONON

Why should I do that? Do you think that I
have any desire for a baby?
By the gods, I only want to be free!
That's the reward I want to take from this.

ONESIMOS

I hope that's what you get.   620

HABROTONON

Then my plotting pleases you?

ONESIMOS

Immeasurably. But if you trick me,
I will fight you and I'll find the means to win.
First let us see if the baby is his.

HABROTONON

We are in agreement?

ONESIMOS

Certainly.

HABROTONON

Then quickly give the ring to me.

ONESIMOS

Take it.

HABROTONON *(taking the ring and speaking a prayer to the goddess of*
                Persuasion)
    Dear Peitho, be allied to me
    and make the words I speak succeed.   630
(Habrotonon goes into the house, leaving Onesimos alone on the stage.)

ONESIMOS
    That girl is something else! When she realized
    that love was not her way to freedom
    (and truly that way is hard on the heart)
    she chose another road. But I will stay a slave
    for a lifetime, sniffling, struck dumb, never
    clever enough to plot out plots like these.
    I may get something from her if she wins.
    That's just just. But I'm debating empty air,
    a luckless fool expecting favors
    from a woman. May my present problem   640
    be enough! For now my mistress is safe,
    but if the mother is a free man's daughter,
    he'll marry her and put aside the wife he has.
    He'll leave behind that crowd inside as well.
    For now, I think I've managed nicely—
    this complication came in spite of me.
    But in the future if you catch me
    nattering or meddling, I offer my balls
    for speedy excision. But who is coming?
    Smikrines is returning from town,   650
    ready to stir up trouble again.
(Smikrines is seen coming onto the stage from the right, heading for
                Charisios' house. He is unaware of Onesimos, who
                continues speaking to the audience for a little
                while.)
    Perhaps he's learned the truth from someone.
    It's better if I get out of his way—
    I surely don't want to chat with him now!
(Onesimos rushes into Chairestratos' house before Smikrines reaches
                center stage.)

SMIKRINES *(to himself, grumbling)*
　　This scandal is talked about all over town.
　　Everyone knows about his drinking bouts
　　and even the name of that harp-girl for hire
　　living with him, while he gambles and spends.
(Karion, the cook, comes angrily out of Chairestratos' house,
　　　　　　　　accompanied by Simias. Smikrines, anxious for
　　　　　　　　information, listens to the cook's complaints, with
　　　　　　　　an occasional aside to the audience.)

KARION
　　What a mess! Give me a house where I
　　can practice my trade without a tirade.　　　　　　　　660
　　Let them go look for some other cook.

SMIKRINES *(aside)*
　　They seem to be enjoying
　　rather a riddling sort of a lunch.

KARION
　　In lots of ways, I'm really unlucky again.
　　All of them now are scattering off,
　　and if anyone asks for the cook to come back,
　　I'll tell him nicely he can go to hell.

SMIKRINES *(aside)*
　　Something really must be happening—
　　the party seems to be over
　　and I wonder what that means.　　　　　　　　　　　　670

KARION
　　So it wasn't enough to play the harp—
　　now she has to be the baby's mother.

SMIKRINES *(rushing up to Karion and speaking to him)*
　　Did you say now there is a baby
　　born to the harp-girl and Charisios?

KARION
  They were eating, and then she bombards them
  with what happened once when he was drinking.
  The final result was the baby.

SMIKRINES
  Can that be true?

KARION
  They have it there.

SMIKRINES
  Dear me, O gods!   680

KARION *(to his assistant Simias, who has come out to join him)*
  I'll send you back for the money later,
  after things have settled down a bit.
  My lady harpist wishes to be mistress
  of this house, O Heracles. Now, let's go.
(Karion and Simias leave. Smikrines is alone on the stage, dumbfounded,
              when Chairestratos comes out and excitedly speaks
              to the audience.)

CHAIRESTRATOS
  Yes, by the Sun, I almost was in love
  with her myself. But now I'd rather die.
  A baby by Charisios! And now
  her eyebrows are raised high and haughty
  as if she's raised herself already
  to be the mistress of his house.   690

SMIKRINES *(overhearing, and rushing up to him)*
  What's that about a baby? You're his friend.
  Do you suppose he is ashamed to be
  the father of a baby by that whore?
  Oh, if only my daughter had a son
  by him instead. Then there'd be a marriage,
  but now they're both unhappy and unlucky.

CHAIRESTRATOS
Certainly unhappy and unlucky,
and the result is chaos in my house.

SMIKRINES
Perhaps you consider me to be
a busybody bothering with more   700
than is my right. But I have reason now
to take my daughter out of here and go.
That's what I'll do, I've just about decided,
and you can be the witness to my words.

CHAIRESTRATOS
Your daughter has been treated badly,
I'll give you no argument there, but still
he hates the life he's living now.

SMIKRINES *(outraged)*
You dare to say he hates the honeyed life
he's leading at your house! He drinks like a wonder,
spends his evenings with that wicked witch   710
and intends to do the same tomorrow.

CHAIRESTRATOS
I think it's better if you stand apart—
please don't rush to judgment in this case.

SMIKRINES
To my misfortune, marriage is the link
between Charisios and me. I'll make him pay!
He thinks he's high and mighty, but he'll fall
with that new beauty in his life. Why soon—
he'll decide to live with a third one too
and still I bet he thinks I'll have no clue.
(Smikrines stomps off to Charisios' house to talk with Pamphile, while
         Chairestratos stands thoughtfully for a few
                  moments and then goes off to the right. Soon after,
                  the besotted chorus appears.)

CHORUS

We drink and sing of various versions   720
of stories conjured from illusions.
Helen never walked the walls of Troy—
the Spartan queen spurned Paris as a boy.
Who can fathom what is real
when it is Aphrodite's deal?
In his prayers Helen's father forgot her praise
and his daughters' lovers suffered in various ways.

ACT IV

*(Pamphile and her father Smikrines come out of Charisios' house in
the middle of an emotional argument. Charisios is seen hiding
by the side of his own house.)*

PAMPHILE

If you don't persuade me, you can't save me—
and you'll be thought my master, not my father.

SMIKRINES

This business doesn't call for words   730
or a meeting of minds. It cries
for action, Pamphile, there's nothing
to argue about. But since I must, I'll speak—
I'm ready to put three things before you—
first, your husband is unredeemable,
and, second, your situation can't improve.
He hasn't a care; he's living it up
while you just wait and let it go on.
Third—have you ever thought of the life
you'd live if you share him with another?   740
Where will all of the money come from?
Think of the waste; he'll have to pay twice
for Demeter's festivals, twice for the
Thesmophoria, and twice again for the Scira.
Now learn about the ruin of your life.
Agree that he will destroy his future

and then consider yourself. How will you feel
if he says that he's at the Piraeus
but he's really messing around with that girl?
You'll run around preparing his dinner   750
while he takes his time drinking with her.
You'll spend your life waiting for nothing.

PAMPHILE

I just can't leave, not yet, I still have hope
that something good may come in spite of this.

SMIKRINES

Pamphile, it's hard for you, a freeborn girl,
to persist in warfare with a whore.
She's good at dirty fighting: she knows more
and has no shame, and she knows how to please.
I'm going now, but think of what I've said.
(*Smikrines heads off stage, toward town. Charisios quietly goes back to
Chairestratos' house. Pamphile is alone and after a
pause, thinks of the trauma she has suffered and
speaks in an aside to the audience.*)

PAMPHILE

My eyes were blurred and burning me—   760
I had been sobbing so hard, and now . . .
(*She pauses as she sees Habrotonon come out of the house carrying the
crying baby, but then turns away, wrapped up in
her own thoughts.*)

HABROTONON (*aloud, to herself, not yet noticing Pamphile*)
I'll take the baby outside with me—
the poor thing has been weeping for so long.
I don't understand what's troubling him.

PAMPHILE (*to herself, continuing*)
Is there a god to pity me
alone here in my misery?

HABROTONON *(to the baby)*
  O dearest child, when will you ever
  set eyes again upon your mother?
  (Habrotonon notices Pamphile and starts with recognition.)

PAMPHILE *(to herself)*
  I suppose I'll go inside again.

HABROTONON *(chasing after Pamphile, calling out to her)*
  My lady, wait a little while.   770

PAMPHILE *(turning back)*
  Are you calling me?

HABROTONON
  Yes, turn around and face me now.

PAMPHILE
  Do you know me?

HABROTONON *(excitedly)*
  You're the very one I saw.
  I greet you, dearest girl.

PAMPHILE *(puzzled)*
  But who are you?

HABROTONON
  Here, give me your hand, and tell me, sweetest—
  last year, were you there to see the sights
  at the Tauropolia with other girls?

PAMPHILE *(looking at the baby)*
  Tell me lady, where you got that baby.   780

HABROTONON
  Tell me dearest, is there something familiar
  in what he's wearing? Please don't be afraid.

PAMPHILE
> Didn't you give birth to him?

HABROTONON
> I pretended that I did. I meant no harm
> to his mother, but I needed the time
> to find her. Now I have—it's you,
> for you're the girl I saw before.

PAMPHILE
> But who is his father?

HABROTONON
> It's Charisios.

PAMPHILE
> Dearest lady, do you know for sure?   790

HABROTONON
> I'm sure. But aren't you his wife,
> and don't you live in there?
> *(points to Charisios' house)*

PAMPHILE
> I do. It's true.

HABROTONON
> A god has taken pity on you both.
> O lady, may you now be happy!
> But now a neighbor's rattling the doors
> and soon will be out here. Bring me in with you
> so you can learn the rest from me at leisure.
> *(Pamphile and Habrotonon go into Charisios' house with the baby.*
> > *Onesimos exits from Chairestratos' house onto the*
> > *stage.)*

ONESIMOS *(to the audience)*
> He's crazy, by Apollo, he's just crazy.
> He truly has gone mad. By the gods, he's mad!   800

I'm referring to Charisios, my master.
He's fallen sick with melancholia—
what else could explain how it is?
That wretched man has just been hiding
a long time near the door to his own house,
to hear his wife speak with her father,
and I can't decently describe to you
how he kept changing color as he spoke.
"O sweetest girl, you say such things" he cried
and then he smacked himself upon his head.   810
Then again he said, "I've a wife like this,
and now see what's happened to me!"
When he finished listening, he ran inside
again, and once inside was howling,
pulling out his hair, really out of his mind.
Heavily, he heaved, "I'm guilty too
and I've committed that same sin myself,
myself, the father of a bastard child
and yet I had no hint of sympathy
for *her* in her misfortune. I'm brutal,   820
heartless . . . "that's how he went on, staring
into space with bloodshot eyes. As for me,
I'm frozen up with fear. I'm drained up, dry.
If he, in rage, should somehow see me here,
he will likely aim his fury right at me—
he might even kill me—that's why I sneaked out
secretly, but where do I to turn now?
What should my plan be? I'm dead, I'm done for—
O Savior Zeus, there's a noise at the door,
he's coming out—so save me if if you can.   830
(Onesimos rushes off stage into Charisios' house. Charisios comes out,
speaking.)

CHARISIOS

As if I were blameless, I considered
my reputation with excessive pride,

judging what is shameful and what's noble—
until I was shattered myself, in my life,
by some god who rightly hit me very hard
and showed me that I'm merely human.
That god as good as said to me "You wretch,
you babble and boast and will not tolerate
the forced misfortune that your wife has faced.
I'll show you how you fell in the same way.   840
Yet she is kind, while you dishonor her
and show yourself to be a stupid brute."
So how did she speak to her father?
She told him that she came to share my life
no matter what misfortune came our way,
and yet I acted so superior.
A god pursues me and I have to stay—
but what will her furious father say?
Oh, why shoud I care about him? I'll say,
"Smikrines, don't bother me, my wife won't leave,   850
so why not stop harassing Pamphile?"
(Onesimos quietly exits from Charisios' house, but Charisios notices him
and speaks to him.)
Why am I looking at you once more?

ONESIMOS *(to Habrotonon, inside)*
I'm in trouble now, I beg you, lady,
please don't leave me stranded here, Oh, dear!

CHARISIOS
Have you been listening, you rotten wretch?

ONESIMOS
I swear, by the gods, I've just come outside.
How can I hide from you, by Zeus—just hear . . .

CHARISIOS
Haven't I seen you sneaking around all the time
with your loud and evil mouth?

ONESIMOS
Let me try to help you now.   860
(Habrotonon comes out of the house and addresses Charisios.)

HABROTONON
You've got to hear—the baby isn't mine.

CHARISIOS
What do you mean? How can he not be yours?

HABROTONON
He's yours. Don't you want to hear the story?

CHARISIOS
Immediately—

HABROTONON
I ought to say . . .

ONESIMOS *(excitedly)*
Yes, you ought to.

CHARISIOS *(becoming confused and angry)*
Are you two in a plot to test me?

ONESIMOS
By Apollo, she persuaded me . . .

HABROTONON *(to Charisios)*
Don't argue, sweetheart, the baby belongs
to your own wife. It's hers, and not another's.   870

CHARISIOS
If only that were true!

HABROTONON
Dearest Demeter, it is!

CHARISIOS (*slowly becoming aware of the possibilities*)
>What are you telling me?

HABROTONON
>Only the truth.

CHARISIOS
>The child of Pamphile? But it was mine.

HABROTONON
>Yes, it's yours as well.

CHARISIOS (*dazed*)
>Pamphile's? I beg you, don't encourage
>me too much. I can't believe it's true.

HABROTONON
>How can I convince you, you poor man?
>But you will come to understand quite soon.   880
>Just wait and hear it all from us inside.

CHARISIOS
>If that's the truth, why did you lie before?

HABROTONON
>I needed to, because I wasn't sure—
>I had to find its mother first.

CHARISIOS
>I understand, I think. You're right, of course.

HABROTONON
>Of course you are confused. Just come inside
>and Pamphile will tell you what occurred.
>(*Habrotonon and Charisios go into Charisios' house. Onesimos slips in
>>with them. Chorus comes out for its last
>>performance.*)

CHORUS

From Mount Olympus Zeus has poured down rain,
but now the day is clear for honeyed wine.
Let's drink beyond capacity and again,   890
and keep it flowing for your guests and mine.

Head for the krater, get your greatest bowl
for wine that is a mirror to the soul.
We'll celebrate our narrow escape from grief
and bind our heads with wreaths of myrtle leaf.

ACT V

*(Chairestratos comes out of his house, unaware of the developments
that have just taken place between Charisios and the women.)*

CHAIRESTRATOS

After all these revelations, consider
yourself, Chairestratos, and how to keep
your friendship with Charisios intact.
He's faithful to me now, just as he was,
and she's no simple playmate stopping by.   900
It's serious, and now she's borne a child.
Also, her mind is like a mind that's free.
Oh, I wish I were at peace. Do not think
about that harp-girl, I still tell myself,
and yet I see the two of them alone,
Charisios, who's dearest now to her,
and I must keep my distance as a friend,
and only hope that I can soon forget her.
I should leave what I can't have, like the wolf
with gaping jaws, who sees what he desires   910
but knows that it is out of reach.
(Onesimos comes out of Chairestratos' house and approaches him.)

ONESIMOS

Amazing how it's all worked out, I'll say!

CHAIRESTRATOS
    Onesimos, do me one small kindness—
    just take yourself away from here.

ONESIMOS
    But don't you want to hear the latest news—
    what Habrotonon has done for us?

CHAIRESTRATOS
    I wish them every joy with their new child.

ONESIMOS
    But how did you find out? It's only now
    the mother of the baby has been found.

CHAIRESTRATOS *(annoyed)*
    Onesimos, where have you been? You saw   920
    not long ago, and at my house, the proofs
    presented to Charisios. Wait now—
    what did you just say? The father was found,
    the mother had her baby with her—there.

ONESIMOS
    But she wasn't really the mother,
    she just had a plan to find the parents.

CHAIRESTRATOS *(increasingly frustrated)*
    Onesimos, make sense. What plan was there
    between Charisios and the harp-girl?

ONESIMOS
    No, not between them. The plan was to find
    the father first and then the mother.   930
    And so, by his ring, she found Charisios,
    and then she happened to see Pamphile
    and recognized her as the girl she'd seen.

CHAIRESTRATOS
> What do you mean—Pamphile?
> What has Pamphile to do with this?

ONESIMOS
> Why, Pamphile's the mother, and the child
> was wearing clothes that she had left with it.

CHAIRESTRATOS
> What about Habrotonon? Does she love
> Charisios? Why did she help them both?
> And also why did she deceive him first?   940
> I'm still not sure if this makes sense to me.

ONESIMOS
> She had to be sure of the father
> before she could try to approach the girl.
> *(Pamphile, holding the baby, Charisios, and Habrotonon come out from*
> *Charisios' house. Chairestratos comes up to them*
> *and speaks to Charisios.)*

CHAIRESTRATOS
> My friend, I hear you found yourself a child
> by your own wife. Can this be the truth?

CHARISIOS *(beaming with happiness)*
> It is. I have. I can hardly believe it—
> Habrotonon has acted now for me
> like a divininty upon the stage
> who brings the lovers together again.
> Pamphile has forgiven me, kindly,   950
> more than I deserve, and I forgive her
> everything, which I should have done before.
> I was angry, but now we're together—
> her father will never take her away.

CHAIRESTRATOS *(dazed)*
    I'm happy for the three of you—I mean
    the baby too—but I need to ask you—
    what about Habrotonon? Will she stay?

HABROTONON *(to Chairestratos)*
    It's time for me to find some other work,
    but I have more than hinted at rewards
    I've hoped for—and I think, Charisios,   960
    that you could buy my freedom and I'd be
    both glad for you and grateful forever.

CHARISIOS *(to Habrotonon)*
    I will see to it that you are free—
    and thanks will always flow to you from me.

ONESIMOS
    But what about me?

CHARISIOS
    Get in the house and be grateful to be
    alive and unharmed. Your blather started
    me on my impetuousity.
(Onesimos makes his way into Charisios' house. Charisios, Pamphile,
                and the baby follow. Habrotonon is on stage with
                Chairestratos.)

CHAIRESTRATOS *(to Habrotonon)*
    If you are soon to be free, do you think
    that I may ask you anyway if you   970
    could play the harp for me, or let me see
    if there is something I might do for you?

HABROTONON
    It never hurts to have some extra friends.

CHAIRESTRATOS
Then let me be your friend and hope that you
will someday think of me as more than friend.
(*Habrotonon smiles at him and they go off into his house together. A few
moments after, Charisios comes out of his house,
planning to speak to Chairestratos. He speaks in an
aside to the audience.*)

CHARISIOS (*with unintended irony*)
I just don't trust him with Habrotonon.
He hasn't any sense of moderation
as I do. If he's left alone with her,
I doubt he'll keep his hands where they belong,
the way I did—for I was chaste with her   980
and treated her respectfully, but he
may not appreciate her properly.
She's been my friend, and I must speak to him . . .
but I must settle my own business first.
(*Charisios goes back into his own house. Then Smikrines enters,
accompanied by his servant, Sophrone.*)

SMIKRINES (*to Sophrone*)
I'll bash your head in for you, Sophrone,
or I'll be damned. Are *you* advising *me*?
You say I'm being rash and impulsive
in taking my daughter back again with me.
You thieving old witch, you think I should wait
until her husband's eaten all my wealth?   990
Why do I only *talk* about what's mine?
Is that what you're advising me—to talk?
It's better if I strike like lightening—
then I'll hear him scream. Are you nattering
at me again, are you my judge, you hag?
Go inside to Pamphile and make her
change her mind, or else—did you see that lake
when we were coming here? I'll drown you there,

I'll hold you under water all night long—
and show you how you must agree with me.   1000
(Smikrines and Sophrone are now at the door of Charisios' house.)
I must bang harder at that door—it's locked.
Hey, slaves—you—boy—someone open up!
Anyone there, I'm speaking now to you!

ONESIMOS *(opening the door and standing in the doorway)*
Who's beating on the door? O Smikrines,
hard-hearted man, are you arriving here
to lay claim to your daughter and dowry?

SMIKRINES
It's me, you damned and blasted fool!

ONESIMOS
Quite right that you do. You're most logical,
by Heracles, you are in such a rush
to steal a dowry—it's quite amazing.   1010

SMIKRINES *(infuriated)*
By the gods and demigods—

ONESIMOS
Do you think the gods have leisure time
to mete out good and bad for everyone
every single day, O Smikrines?

SMIKRINES
What in the hell are you talking about?

ONESIMOS *(smugly)*
I'll teach you and I'll make it very clear.
There are about a thousand cities—and
some thirty thousand people live in them.
Can the gods be bothered to save or damn

each individual? Ridiculous!   1020
That way you'd wear them out on us like slaves!
They've given us each a guardian
inside us, and it watches if we treat
another badly, and guards *him* if we do.
That god is in each of us, responsible
for whether we act badly or well.
In order to get on, don't be a fool
and stop making stupid mistakes.

SMIKRINES *(baffled and outraged)*
You rotten thief, do you call me a fool?

ONESIMOS
It's wears you down and it grinds you away.   1030

SMIKRINES
Of all the nerve!

ONESIMOS
So do you judge it right to act with force
and make you daughter leave her husband now?

SMIKRINES
We're not even talking of what's right,
I'm saying that it must be done.

ONESIMOS *(speaking to Sophrone)*
You see how he reasons? "Must" he calls it
when what he "must" do is clearly evil.
His personality's destroying him.
(to Smikrines)
And you, you were all set to make a mess
of everything, but chance has saved you this time.   1040
and you've arrived to find those problems solved.
But Smikrines, don't let me catch you again

rushing headlong where you don't belong.
Stop your complaining and take your daughter's . . .
baby who is here inside this house.

SMIKRINES
    My daughter's *baby*! You ought to be whipped!

ONESIMOS *(placidly)*
    Your head was so thick, you thought you knew it all—
    so how did you guard your girl before she married?
    that's how we find that we must care for freaks—
    or babies that are four months premature.   1050

SMIKRINES *(puzzled and aghast)*
    I have no clue—I can't sort out the sense . . .

ONESIMOS
    But your old nurse can do it, I believe.
(to Sophrone)
    At the Tauropolia, my master
    took the girl away from all the dancing—
    didn't he?
(to Smikrines)
    So now you understand it.
    Yes, and now they've recognized each other
    and everything has turned out well for them

SMIKRINES *(to Sophrone, with anger)*
    You thieving old woman, what do you say?

ONESIMOS *(interjecting)*
    "It was Nature's will and laws were no use,   1060
    for woman was born for such a purpose."
    That's Euripides, you fool, do I need
    to quote the "Auge" to you word for word?
    Remember Auge, raped by Heracles,

went on to have his child. He left a ring,
and that's how his identity was found.
The same thing has happened to your Pamphile.

SMIKRINES *(to Sophrone)*
You knew this all along—you wretched hag—
You know exactly what he's telling me!

ONESIMOS
She knows, believe me, she knew all along.   1070

SMIKRINES
What you've said—it shakes me up completely!

ONESIMOS
But nothing's ever turned out better.

SMIKRINES *(softening)*
If you're telling me the truth, the child then
is my grandson, though he was conceived too soon.
I still don't understand—missing pieces
puzzle me, and all this plotting, while I
was plodding back and forth to get my daughter back.
How could this have happened to her?
Did I fail her in some way? Am I mad,
a fool, or just obtuse? I didn't know—   1080
although that nurse and she conspired
to hide the facts from me, her father.
I must adjust—it may not be too late
to see her happy with Charisios.

CHARISIOS *(appearing in the doorway of the house with Pamphile)*
Father, please come in and speak with us—
we can't pretend there never was a problem—
but we've resolved it now and want to have
your blessing. Come inside and meet the child.

We do admit that shameful things have happened,
but shame and pain are part of being human, 1090
and we must now begin to do what's right.
The baby was born free, he will be raised
with all nobility, and free from scorn.

SMIKRINES *(going inside)*
    All may yet go well, the child is my own
    grandchild, and he's probably the one I saved
    from that sneaky shepherd grubbing his belongings.
    That charcoal-burner should have some reward—
    he guessed the child had parents who were free.
    And now I'll try to keep Charisios
    responsible financially from this day on. 1100

ONESIMOS
    I'm off the hook, they're happy, I am free—
    well, not completely free, but free of cares
    and free to speak and act and celebrate.
    I'll go and get that cook back to this house—
    and start the preparations for a party—
    in honor of the union with their baby.
(to the audience)
    So favor us now with your applause,
    then come and share the feast with us indoors!

Closely Cropped Locks (Perikeiromene)

Translated by
Sheila D'Atri and Palmer Bovie

Passion, the possibility of incest, and violence on the home-front are the topical topics in this domestic tragicomedy. Human weaknesses (mostly male) strut and fret upon the stage and all comes out right in the end.

Of course we know this at the beginning. The goddess Ignorance herself has stirred up the pot and the characters so that the truth might be ultimately known. Again, we have to go into the past to get to the beginning (and omniscient prologue divinities are very good at supplying history as well as answers). Long, long ago, about eighteen years ago, a man lost his wife and then his wealth and then his equilibrium. He had his twin babies— a boy and a girl—exposed and they were rescued. (Where would the drama be if they weren't?) An old woman found them but was too poor to raise two children and so gave the boy to a wealthy woman who wanted a son. Of course they move next door, but not before the old woman, on the point of death, tells her adopted daughter who her brother is. This is a precaution against unwitting incest, and she also feels that this brother may be a help in time of need.

Need him? He is the beginning of all her troubles, a lecherous pest. Meanwhile, she has been living with a Corinthian soldier, jealous and hot-headed, who comes home to find the neighbor embracing his girl. How could she have pushed him away? Her only brother! But how can she speak? To tell of their relationship would ruin his social standing. She does not deign to explain. Polemon the soldier goes into a rage and cuts off her hair with his sword. (Hence the title of this play, literally "the girl with the cut-off hair.") Now she complains bitterly and leaves him, outraged at this last example of brutish behavior. She finds refuge with her neighbor, the adopted mother of her brother Moschion. Moschion's mother is clearly in the know—and keeps her lovesick son away. He sulks in his room in confusion and despair, since somehow he had convinced himself that his mother was providing him with the girlfriend of his dreams. He was wrong!

What else is in this tangled web? Polemon the soldier is contrite—more than contrite: he is devastated and keeps on sending his servant Sosias to find out what is going on at the home front. Meanwhile, Sosias manages to get into some quasi-battles with Daos, the slave of Moschion, who has been encouraging his master in hope of gain.

Then Pataikos arrives, an elderly man (the unrevealed father), who serves as friend to Polemon. He gives Polemon more advice than sympathy—if he is not legally married, the woman has the right to leave him if she is not treated properly. Polemon, anxious to justify himself and have Pataikos plead his case with Glykera (Sweetie), begs him to see the clothing he has given her. The warlike hero starts to show a touchingly domestic side, and seems less and less like an abuser. Even so, Pataikos has an uphill fight trying to convince her to return. The critical action occurs when Glykera has her servant bring out a chest that holds her baby things. In a scene reminiscent of recognition scenes in tragedy, Pataikos recognizes the embroidery as the work of his late wife and they question each other as Moschion listens, hiding in the wings. (Just before, eavesdropping on his mother, Moschion has discovered that both he and Glykera are foundlings.) The three are soon happily reconciled, although Moschion greets his sister with mixed emotions.

All that is left is to resolve the conflict between Glykera and Polemon. The tame, reformed Polemon is finally forgiven. Since Glykera has found her father, she has citizen status and can marry. Pataikos is delighted to officiate—at two weddings, not just one. Moschion will settle down and marry the daughter of his friend.

Cast

POLEMON, a soldier
GLYKERA, his mistress
SOSIAS, his slave
DORIS, Glykera's maid
AGNOIA, goddess of Ignorance or Misapprehension
MOSCHION, a young man
DAOS, Moschion's slave
CHORUS of young revelers
PATAIKOS, the unknown father of Moschion and Glykera
HABROTONON, a harp-girl
NONSPEAKING
    Servants
    Myrrhine, Moschion's adoptive mother

*(The action takes place on a street in Corinth, before the houses of
    Myrrhine and Polemon. Pataikos' house is nearby, offstage. The
    street leads on the left to the marketplace in the city and on the
    right to the countryside.)*

ACT I

*(The first scene opens in the middle of a violent dispute between
    Polemon and Glykera. Glykera's hair has been shorn off in a
    lopsided way. She is upset and angry, while Polemon, apologetic,
    is trying to calm her and woo her back. Glykera's maid Doris is
    standing out of the way.)*

POLEMON
    But I saw that rascal kissing you
    and you did nothing, not protesting.
    I saw you there with Moschion
    and when I came near and saw you closer,
    I hardly believed my eyes . . .

GLYKERA *(crying)*
>You should believe me! You still don't know
>whatever it was that you think you saw.

POLEMON
>Then tell me, dearest, what is the reason
>you didn't resist? I'll try to understand.

GLYKERA
>There's nothing more for me to say.   10
>I told you it was no concern of yours.
>Anyway you stormed away from me,
>and then rampaging back, disgusting, drunk,
>you grabbed my hair and sheared it with your sword.

POLEMON *(pleading)*
>Glykera, honey, why are you crying?
>I swear by Zeus and Mount Olympus
>and also by Athena, dearest one—
>I do esteem and trust and love you,
>and what I did was wrong. I'm sorry now.

GLYKERA
>You've sworn before, and many times before   20
>there's always been a reason for your rage.
>I've been humiliated long enough—
>I'm leaving. Don't expect me back.

POLEMON
>I shouldn't have done it—the embrace
>I witnessed was harmless enough, and yet
>I worked myself up into a temper.
>Your hair will all grow back. Don't go away—
>I know what I did was an offense to you,
>but you still look beautiful to me.

GLYKERA *(determined)*
>   It doesn't matter what you say,   30
>   I don't care how I look to you,
>   I'm leaving for Myrrhine's house—
>   don't even try to talk to me again.

(Glykera and Doris take bundles of belongings to the house next door, where Myrrhine, waiting, lets them in.)

POLEMON *(alone on stage)*
>   I've got to win her back, I love her, but
>   I had a right to feel suspicious—
>   for after all, she didn't push him off.
>   I wish that I had never seen that man,
>   that Moschion, hanging around my house.
>   But cutting off her hair was cruel.
>   I should have thought . . . I didn't think . . .   40
>   but now I only know I want her back.

(Polemon goes dejectedly into his house. When the stage is clear, the goddess Agnoia enters to explain the situation to the audience.)

AGNOIA
>   I am the Goddess of Misapprehension.
>   Misunderstanding is often the reason
>   people come into terrible conflict.
>   There is a complicated situation here.
>   Many years ago, about eighteen,
>   the wife of Pataikos died in childbirth
>   after giving birth to twins—Glykera
>   and Moschion. Grieving, Pataikos
>   learned his ship had sunk with all his fortune.   50
>   He sent his servant to expose the twins,
>   finding it impossible to raise them
>   beggared and without a wife.
>   A poor old woman found the babies.
>   She could not keep them both, but she knew someone,

Myrrhine, a wealthy woman,
who lives here and who wished to raise a son.
So she gave him up and kept the girl herself.
Eventually, they all will know the truth,
but for now Misapprehension rules the day.   60
Back to our story. Eighteen years later,
after the long, hard wars, Corinthian
life got harder to bear for the poor.
And so the old woman who raised the girl
(the one you just saw here) gave her over—
as if she were truly her daughter—
to a lover, that rash young soldier,
Corinthian born, named Polemon.
That was the best she could do for her.
After all, there was no dowry for the girl.   70
By now the old woman was failing,
but, foreseeing the uncertainties of life,
she told the girl how she happened to find her
and gave her the clothes and trinkets she'd worn.
She also told her—she'd never known before—
of her brother by birth, who happens to live next door.
She told her, in case she ever needed help,
and also to prevent the chance of incest
that might come through ignorance,
so she might be on guard, lest innocent   80
(through me, Misapprehension, ruling),
she take her brother as her lover.
That young man Moschion is rather rich
and also given to excessive drinking,
while she is young and lovely, and her tie
to Polemon is not a marriage bond.
Then the old woman died, and, soon after,
the soldier bought the house you see right here.
So the girl became the neighbor of her brother,
but hasn't said a thing to anyone,   90
afraid to damage his social position

if it were known he was her relative.
Well, quite by chance he saw her—and he's bold,
as I just mentioned—so he's always
wandering around beside her house.
Yesterday evening she was at the door,
sending her maid on an errand,
and as soon as he saw her standing there,
he rushed up and hugged her and kissed her,
while she, knowing he was her brother,   100
couldn't bring herself to run away.
Then the soldier came and saw them there.
What happened next you can guess—Polemon
was furious, marched off, and said they'd talk
"when she could spare the time." Then he returned
with all his pent-up rage, while she just cried
because she wasn't free to greet her brother.
I intended this to make Polemon burn—
I drove him on beyond his nature—
that everything might someday be revealed.   110
If anyone is disgusted at this
or thinks that I have been too hard,
turn it 'round and think about it again.
what's done by a god is good in the end.
Audience be kind, and change your minds.
Watch the rest of the play, and and may you all prosper.
*(The goddess exits to the left, while Sosias, Polemon's slave, enters on the
right.)*

SOSIAS *(complaining)*
That blustering and warlike master
of mine—the one who won't allow a girl
to keep her hair—is lying on the ground
and crying, while all his friends console him.   120
I've just left them at their breakfast—he has
no way of knowing what is going on
at home and so he sent me here to get his cloak.

He doesn't really want the cloak, he wants
to keep me running about like a slave.
(Doris, Glykera's maid, comes out of Polemon's house, speaking to
Glykera at the door.)

DORIS
I'll go and get things ready, my lady.

SOSIAS *(aside, to the audience)*
It's Doris! She's looking like she's living well.
They both are, I bet. I'd better get going.
(Sosias goes into Polemon's house to fetch the cloak. It becomes apparent
to him that Glykera is intending to move out.
Meanwhile, Doris approaches Myrrhine's door.)

DORIS
I'll knock on the door.
(knocks)
                          Is anyone there?
Whatever woman takes a soldier   130
for a lover has my sympathy.
They all think they're above the law
and none deserve your trust. My mistress
has done nothing wrong, but she's been wronged by him.
(knocks at the door again)
Slaves, open up!
(The door opens and Doris goes inside carrying some objects. Meanwhile,
Sosias comes out from from Polemon's house
carrying the cloak.)

SOSIAS
He'll be happy to learn she's crying now—
that's just what he wanted to hear.
(Sosias goes off to the right. Doris comes out of Myrrhine's house and
meets up with Glykera. Daos comes onto the stage
from the left, where he has been in town with
Moschion. He stays hidden, watching and listening
to the women.)

DORIS

    Myrrhine's ready for you, mistress—
    she's full of sympathy and will treat you
    as a daughter. You can stay there   140
    as long as you like and feel at ease.

GLYKERA

    I'm lucky to find such a lady—
    I'll never go back to Polemon,
    but I'm not sure how long I'll be able to stay.
(She knocks at the door of Myrrhine's house.)
    Slaves, open up, let us in.
(Glykera and Doris go into the house. Daos comes to the center of the
stage and addresses the audience.)

DAOS *(pleased, but deluded as to the meaning of Myrrhine's motives)*
    My master will be delighted at the news!
    Never has a mother been so helpful
    to a son in pursuit of a girl!
    She's actually bringing her here for him—
    and that soldier can't stop it at all.   150
    I'll hurry up and bring Moschion home.
    But this is the time to get out of the way
    of that troop of young drunks who are coming.
(Daos goes off to fetch Moschion, while the chorus of young drunks
makes its first entr'acte appearance.)

CHORUS

    Returning from the bronze-sounding trumpet,
    our mighty cloaked soldier with massive sword
    comes home to his own beloved strumpet,
    swaggering, seeing himself as a lord.
    Trusting travelers Sciron found—
    they washed his feet without a sound.
    As payment he kicked them over the rocks—   160
    there's worse things in life than losing your locks.

ACT II

(*Moschion and Daos enter the stage from the right. They are in the middle of a conversation.*)

MOSCHION

    Daos, you've lied to me many times before,
    you're a cheat and the gods must detest you.
    And if now you're leading me round in circles . . .

DAOS

    Beat me immediately, if I am cheating.

MOSCHION

    That's what you say today.

DAOS

    Then declare war, if it's not truly so
    that the girl is inside. And if she is,
    what will you do for me then?
    I used all my powers of persuasion   170
    to get her here for you, and then I had
    your mother to convince to take her in
    and make the best arrangements, all for you.
    How will I stand, Moschion, if that's true?

MOSCHION

    See what will please you, Daos, the most—
    what sort of life would you like—what would fit
    your character the best? Do tell me now.

DAOS

    Running a mill may be the best I get.

MOSCHION

    Running in the mill—that should work out well.

DAOS

    Let's not talk about really hard work!   180

MOSCHION *(sarcastically)*

    No, I'll make you chief of all the business
    that's of supreme importance to the Greeks.
    Or maybe I'll make you the head of an army.

DAOS

    Oh, no! They'll slit my throat if they should find
    me larcenous at the arsenal.

MOSCHION

    Oh, you should find a fortune, I should think—
    seven easy talents for a job like that!

DAOS

    Moschion, I have no need to be rich—
    a small store would do—I'd deal in foodstuff.
    A shop in the agora selling cheese—   190
    I swear that would smell good to me.

MOSCHION

    You'd be like the old lady who sells us honey?
    The money would stick to your hands.

DAOS

    You know how fond I am of eating well—
    I deserve those just deserts for what I did—
    you'll see your reward and then give me mine.

MOSCHION

    Let it be so, and you can sell your cheese.

DAOS

    That's what I prayed for, as I said to you,
    now Master, go and open up the door.

MOSCHION

So now I must go in and chat with her   200
and laugh, while you, my military hero
just lately hated by the gods, fly off.

DAOS

Why certainly.

MOSCHION

Daos, I want you to go inside first,
and look around at all that's happening.
What is the girl doing, where is my mother,
and how are they likely to greet me?
I don't have to tell you every detail,
I want you to tell me. Go on, you're no fool.

DAOS

I'm on my way.   210
(*Daos goes up to Myrrhine's house and prepares to go inside.*)

MOSCHION

I'll walk back and forth in front of the house,
and wait for you, Daos, to give me the news.
(*Daos goes inside the house. Moschion speaks in an aside to the audience.*)
Yesterday evening she showed some real feeling—
she didn't run off when I came up to her,
but put her arms around me. I must say
I'm not so unattractive to the girls.
I believe, by Athena, they're all drawn to me.

DAOS (*coming out of Myrrhine's house*)
Moschion, she's bathed and sitting pretty.

MOSCHION

Oh, that darling girl!

DAOS

    Your mother is busy about the house   220
    I don't know what, but the mid-day meal
    is ready, and it seems to me that they're
    only waiting for you to arrive there.

MOSCHION *(smugly)*

    Well, I've known for long that I'm attractive.
    Did you tell them that I'm here?

DAOS

    No, by Zeus.

MOSCHION

    So go and tell them, then!

DAOS

    I'm on my way already.
(Daos goes back into the house.)

MOSCHION

    She'll be modest when I first go in,
    and veil herself, for that's their nature.   230
    As for my mother, when I first come in
    I must kiss her, to win her over
    altogether and keep her fond of me.
    She's shown the most proper feelings for me
    in all that has been happening.
    There's a noise at the door—someone's coming.
    What's this, boy? Daos, you're hesitating.
    Come and tell me what the problem is.

DAOS *(extremely uncomfortable)*

    Good grief, by Zeus, everything's a mess.
    When I came to tell your mother you were here,   240
    she said, "Nothing of that sort around here,"

and "How did my son come to hear of this?
Did *you* babble it all to him and say
how she came here since she was afraid?"
Then she said, "You must have seen it all;
it's all *your* doing, you meddlesome wretch.
Now, boy, get out of my way." Victory
was almost ours, and now it's snatched away.
She wasn't glad to hear you were at hand.

MOSCHION (*angry*)
    You whipping-post, you've cheated me!   250

DAOS (*trying to look nonchalant*)
    What a laugh. It was your mother, not me.

MOSCHION (*frustrated, still angry*)
    What are you talking about? You heard her!
    Yet you had the nerve to tell me
    that she came willingly—for me!
    You also told me you persuaded her
    to come because of me—didn't you now?

DAOS
    I told you *I* persuaded her, not me!
    By Apollo, master, I wouldn't lie to you.

MOSCHION
    A little while ago you said that you
    persuaded my mother to take her in,   260
    and all for my sake, all for me alone!

DAOS
    Yes, I said it, I remember now.

MOSCHION
    You said you thought she did it all for me!

DAOS
     I can't say *that*—but I tried to persuade her.

MOSCHION
     Well then, just walk over . . . closer now.

DAOS *(fearful)*
     Where? Not so far—wait—let me think!

MOSCHION *(grabbing him)*
     You're making an idiot of me.

DAOS *(struggling)*
     By Aesculapius, I wouldn't do that . . .
     just listen to me for a minute.
     You see, perhaps she doesn't want to rush: 270
     you've got to get to know her first.
     She is no call-girl off the streets, by Zeus!
     She can't be treated like a hired flute girl
     or come here like a wretched prostitute.

MOSCHION *(relenting)*
     Daos, now you're making sense again.

DAOS
     Think about it, you know how it is—
     she's just left home and Polemon today—
     I'm not babbling—if you only wait
     three days, maybe four, she'll come around.
     That's what I was told, and now you need to know.   280

MOSCHION *(pensive)*
     Where can I tie you up and leave you, Daos?
     You make my head go round in circles.
     You lied, and now I think you're nattering again.

DAOS

> You won't let me think without disturbing me.
> So now go in and behave properly.

MOSCHION

> And you will run off and leave me to stew?

DAOS *(sarcastically)*

> Certainly—with all the means I have to travel!

MOSCHION

> Come in with me and maybe you can help.

DAOS *(breathing a little easier)*

> Most willingly—I'd love to go with you.

MOSCHION

> Somehow I agree with you—you've won.   290

(Moschion goes into Myrrhine's house with Daos about to follow.)

DAOS

> By a hair, by Heracles! It's harder
> than I thought to work a scheme like this.

(Sosias enters with a cloak and a sword, and does not see Daos.)

SOSIAS *(grumbling)*

> Here I am, back with his sword and his cloak
> as pretext for looking around the place
> and then to return and tell him what I find.
> I'm tempted to tell him I found Moschion,
> the adulterer caught in Polemon's house—
> that would make him jump up and run!
> But still I pity him. I've never seen
> him so pathetic. It's a nightmare.   300
> Oh, it's a bitter homecoming for him.

*(Sosias goes into Polemon's house. Daos comes out from the alley between
the two houses, where he has been watching and
listening.)*

DAOS

    The householder's coming home soon, it seems.

    This business is becoming very hard

    to manage, by Apollo! If his master

    comes back soon from the countryside,

    I think there'll be a row when he appears.

SOSIAS *(coming out of the house, calling back to a slave inside, while Daos*
                   hides again)

    You let her *out*, you cursed low-life!

    You really let her get out of the door!

DAOS

    The man is raging—let me get away again.

(Daos returns to his hiding place.)

SOSIAS

    I bet she's gone to the neighbor's house,   310

    over there where that adulterer lives,

    and is telling us to wail our brains out,

    long and hard, she doesn't care a bit.

DAOS *(to the audience)*

    It seems the soldier has a soothsayer

    in his retinue. He's got it right.

SOSIAS *(approaching Myrrhine's house)*

    Now I'll knock on the neighbor's door.

DAOS *(coming out of hiding)*

    Hey you, you damn-blasted fellow there,

    what is it you want? Why have you come?

SOSIAS

    What? Do you come from this house over here?

DAOS

    Maybe. Is it any business of yours?   320

SOSIAS

> Have you gone out of your mind, by the gods?
> Do you hold a free-born woman by force
> and dare to shut her away from the man
> who happens to be her legal guardian?

DAOS

> What a wicked bootlicker you are.

SOSIAS

> You think we have no stomach for a fight?
> You think we aren't *men* you're dealing with?

DAOS

> Yes, by Zeus, four-obol men, and when
> he and his lot of double drachma hirelings
> come out to fight, we'll beat you easily.   330

SOSIAS

> By Heracles, what nerve! Do you admit
> you have her, then? Come and tell me now.

DAOS

> Get yourself off and going, friend.

SOSIAS *(shouting)*

> Hilarion! Damn him, he's gone.
> *(grabs a slave standing near)*
> Hey you, you can be our witness now.
> *(to Daos)*
> So, do you agree you have the girl?

DAOS *(looking imperturbable)*

> There's no one here.

SOSIAS

> I'll see you sobbing sometime soon. Tell me,
> who do you think you're playing around with?

Who do you think you are fooling?   340
We'll wreck your wretched little house.
Go tell the lover to put on his armor.

DAOS

Poor wretch, you're wasting your time
imagining her to be here in this house.

SOSIAS

My men will spit on your house and blow it down,
the ones you dared to call "four-obol men."

DAOS

I'm joking with you, you dirty dung-eater.

SOSIAS *(insulted)*

This—is this considered civilized talk?

DAOS

I've said it. We don't have her.

SOSIAS

I'm going to get my fourteen-foot spear—   350
my Macedonian weapon.

DAOS

Go to hell, I don't care what you do!
I am going inside.
(goes into Myrrhine's house)

DORIS *(coming out of Myrrhine's house as Daos is going in)*
Sosias! It's you!

SOSIAS

Doris, if you come near me, I'll see
that you come to serious harm.
You're the cause of all our problems.

DORIS
>   Please, now, go tell him that she's fled in fear
>   to a lady friend of hers.

SOSIAS *(disbelieving)*
>   In fear? She fled to a *female* friend?   360

DORIS
>   Yes, she's gone to Myrrhine, her neighbor,
>   and that's what I would wish for her.

SOSIAS
>   So that's where she's gone — to where her sweetheart lives?

DORIS
>   Sosias, she's not doing what you think.

SOSIAS
>   Take yourself out of my way, you and your lies.

DORIS
>   I'm going, and you go report what I said.
>   *(Doris goes back into Myrrhine's house, as Sosias turns away to head*
>   *back to Polemon. When the stage is empty, the*
>   *Chorus reappears for the second entr'acte*
>   *performance.)*

CHORUS
>   He drinks up the river of Peneius
>   as if it were a bowl of unmixed wine,
>   oversteps the boundaries with a vengeance.
>   The Vale of Tempe turns to tears in time.   370

ACT III

>   *(Sosias enters with Polemon, followed by an elderly man, Pataikos,*
>   *who lives nearby, and then by Habrotonon, a harp-girl, and*
>   *servants. Sosias is walking unsteadily, obviously drunk. Pataikos*
>   *is trying to give advice to an intoxicated and angry Polemon.)*

SOSIAS *(pointing at Pataikos)*
    Trust me, master, he's taken money
    from the enemy. He has betrayed you
    and all of us in your army.

PATAIKOS *(steadily, to Sosias)*
    Go away and go to sleep, you fool.
    Let it go: you're sick, and making no sense.
(to Polemon)
    It's clear you're not as drunk as your servant.
    Maybe I can reason a bit with you.

POLEMON *(protesting)*
    What do you mean by "not as drunk as him"?
    I've hardly touched more than a cup of wine.
    Miserable as I was, I did foresee   380
    the problems that were bound to happen
    and kept my mind clear for the battle.

PATAIKOS
    So far, so good—now listen to me—

POLEMON *(interrupting)*
    So then, what are you asking me to do?

SOSIAS *(shouting to the harp-girl)*
    Habrotonon—now signal the attack!

PATAIKOS *(to Polemon)*
    Tell them all to go inside the house—
    then I'll be able to have a word with you.

SOSIAS *(to Pataikos)*
    You advise us very badly—we'll lose.
(to Polemon, slurring his words)
    He wants us to disband our army,
    just as we're about to take the force—the fort.   390

POLEMON *(to Sosias)*
>Now wait, you see, this man . . .

SOSIAS *(interrupting)*
>Pataikos? He'll destroy us, leaderless . . .

PATAIKOS *(pushing Sosias out of the way)*
>By the gods, man, go away!

SOSIAS *(to Polemon)*
>I'm going off.
(to the others)
>>>Habrotonon, I hoped
>that you would take some action for us all.
>After all, you're good at climbing up
>and used to circling 'round your target.
(She turns away from him.)
>What! Are you embarrassed by this talk?
>Does it really bother you so much?
(Habrotonon goes off stage in a huff, followed by the other servants.
>>*Sosias dejectedly totters over to the house, flops
>>down, and dozes off.)*

PATAIKOS
>Now, Polemon, as for what happened: 400
>if you were speaking of a marriage vow
>and a woman you were legally bound to . . .

POLEMON *(interrupting)*
>Watch out what you are saying, Pataikos!

PATAIKOS
>Well, it does make a difference, you know.

POLEMON *(angrily)*
>I have thought of her as my legal wife.

PATAIKOS

Don't shout. Who gave the bride away?

POLEMON

Who did? She gave herself to me herself.

PATAIKOS

So far, so good. Perhaps you pleased her then.
Now the situation's changed—she has gone
because she dislikes your behavior now.   410

POLEMON

What are you saying? She hates my behavior?
Saying that, you've really wounded me.

PATAIKOS

You love her—that's clear to me. So why now
are you trying to get her back by force?
Where will you bring her? How will you treat her?
The woman is the mistress of herself.
Persuading her's the only thing to do,
no matter how you love her and want her.

POLEMON

And the man who has corrupted her
when I was gone, wasn't he unjust to me?   420

PATAIKOS

Yes, he was wrong and you can charge with words.
But if you use force and he presses charges,
you'll lose. File a complaint—that you can do.

POLEMON

I can't just flatten him now?

PATAIKOS

No, you can't.

POLEMON *(beside himself)*
>I don't know what I'm saying, by Demeter!
>I'm just about ready to go hang myself.
>Glykera has left me, she's left me—
>Glykera. Pataikos, what can I do?
>Perhaps you can think of something for me to do.   430
>You've talked with her before. Go to her now
>as a sort of ambassador from me.
>I'm begging you, go and talk to her.

PATAIKOS
>I am glad to do this for you.

POLEMON
>You'll know how to present the case for me.

PATAIKOS
>Moderately well, I think.

POLEMON
>Pataikos, you must. In a matter like this,
>you can be a savior to me.
>Oh, if I ever once mistreated her,
>I'll love and honor her from this time on.   440
>Come now and see the jewels I bought her.

PATAIKOS *(demurring)*
>Oh, it's fine as it is.

POLEMON
>Just have a look, Pataikos, by the gods!
>Then you'll have more sympathy for me.

PATAIKOS
>Oh, by Poseidon! You're impossible.

POLEMON *(taking his arm and heading for his house)*
>Come this way with me. The clothes she has here,
>and how she looks when she puts them on . . .
>You've got to see it for yourself.

PATAIKOS
>I have already.

POLEMON
>And her stature was a joy to behold—   450
>Oh why, in the middle of this, do I speak
>about her height? I've been struck dumb, babbling.

PATAIKOS
>By Zeus, you are.

POLEMON
>I am? But, Pataikos, you've got to see
>this finery for yourself. Come with me.

PATAIKOS
>All right, I'll come with you.
>*(He leads Pataikos into his house. As they are going inside, Moschion*
>>*comes out of his mother's house and calls after*
>>*them.)*

MOSCHION
>Go, run away as fast as you can!
>You with your mighty spears in your hands—
>they couldn't even capture the nest
>of a swallow. Daos told me of their hired   460
>soldiers, and their army seems to consist
>of Sosias snoozing alone here.
>*(Pataikos and Polemon have shut the door behind them and Moschion*
>>*then addresses the audience.)*

Of all the miserable people in this world,
no one is more unhappy than I am.
When I went inside, I didn't do
what I usually do. Didn't go
and approach my mother, didn't send for slaves
to bring me anything. I just lay down
by myself in my room.
Then I sent Daos to my mother   470
to tell her I was here. Just that, no more.
They were eating their meal, and Daos here
without a thought of me, sat down and ate.
After some time, just lying by myself,
I thought, "Soon my Mother will send me
a message from my love, telling me how
I might go and meet with her." I thought it,
but nothing happened. At last I was bored
with lying and waiting, and so I went
quietly over to listen in on   480
what they were saying that pertained to me.
By Zeus, I'm in shock, I wasn't prepared
at all for what I heard. First, I found out
that my Mother isn't my mother at all!
She was telling the girl—she never told me—
that I was just a foundling, adopted
by her as a baby. She spoke to her
confidingly, with sympathy for her,
treating her as a respectable girl.
She knew that Glykera was adopted too.   490
That makes her my equal, I suppose—
not just a soldier's hetaira for hire.
I've got to have time to think this over.
Maybe she won't have me as her lover.
Maybe she's really befriended my mother . . .
And where would that leave me? Damnable Daos
misled me again. He never pleaded with mother
for me. He's eating with them and he wants

a little foodstore from me. I'll kill him!
I can't trust him at all. He raised my hopes   500
for the girl I desire hopelessly.
Oh, I'd better get out of the way.
A troop of carousers is coming,
and I have trouble enough for one day.

(Moschion goes off, and the chorus enters for its third performance.)

CHORUS

Theseus claimed he was Poseidon's son
while Minos claimed descent from mighty Zeus.
Minos threw his ring into the ocean,
but Theseus then dove and pried it loose.
Among the rocks his ring had caught his eye—
a jewel worn by lustful Pasiphae.   510

ACT IV

(Pataikos comes out from Polemon's house and addresses the audience before knocking on the door of Myrrhine's house.)

PATAIKOS *(with exasperation)*

I promised Polemon, but what am I?
Who am I to question or counsel her?
She knows me as a neighbor and she knows
I'm not the sort to meddle, but I must,
since after all, I promised Polemon
I'd try to find the reason for her flight.

(He knocks on the door of Myrrhine's house. A slave opens the door and stands there.)

I'd like to speak to Glykera. Tell her
that it's her neighbor Pataikos.
She knows me and I know she won't refuse.

(After a few minutes, while Pataikos is pacing around, Glykera comes to the door.)

GLYKERA *(puzzled)*

Pataikos, what is your business with me?   520

PATAIKOS

I've come to speak on behalf of a friend,
one who loves you and is full of regrets.

GLYKERA

If it's Polemon you're speaking for,
you're wasting your breath and my time.

PATAIKOS

But after all the hours you spent with him,
doesn't he deserve at least a hearing?

GLYKERA

Look at my hair! Did I deserve this?
He should have taken time to talk with me—
before becoming madly, raving drunk,
and then actually assaulting me.   530

PATAIKOS

He knows that now. He was out of control.
He asked that I approach you for some answers.
You need answer only what you want to.
But really, the man is mad with grief now.
Be generous and talk with me a while.

GLYKERA *(resigned)*

All right then, ask, what does he want to know?

PATAIKOS

Did you come here to be near Moschion?

GLYKERA *(exasperated, protesting)*

My dear old friend, could you possibly think
I'd run to his own mother for rescue?
You're not being logical at all!   540
Do you think he would take me as his wife?

Not likely! In his position he'd hardly
marry a girl with a background like mine.
Do you think he'd want me as a hetaira?
Then he himself would want to conceal
such an arrangement from his family,
and so would I. So, rashly, then,
he's brought me here to his own father's house,
while I've been foolish enough to make myself
a hated, awkward burden to his mother.   550
Pataikos, wouldn't I feel full of shame
to behave that way?
But it seems that you came here with that thought
in your mind. Were you persuaded, then,
that *that* was what sort you could take me for?

PATAIKOS

By Zeus, I honor what you say to me—
I believe you. But is there some proof?

GLYKERA *(annoyed)*

No matter what you think, go back to him
and tell him to find some other girl
to abuse the next time he goes crazy.   560

PATAIKOS

Was it really so absolutely awful?

GLYKERA *(interrupting)*

Yes, absolutely—look at me—what sort
of low-class girl would I be taken for?

PATAIKOS

You're right—that chopped-off hair does make you look
like a slave or a cheap prostitute.
I admit that he's shamed you. He has no excuse,
but he loves you and jealousy rules him.

GLYKERA *(proudly)*
> My honor is at stake. Let him suffer
> for what he did to me. I have my pride,
> I am no slave. I was born poor but free.   570
> I have some objects to prove what I'm saying,
> things the old lady who raised me gave me,
> that would prove who my mother by birth
> and my true father were, if they ever saw them.
> I keep these items always by my side.
> Now is your chance to do something for me.

PATAIKOS
> All right then, what do you want?

GLYKERA
> Get them out of that house and bring them here.

PATAIKOS
> You mean you're leaving him for good?
> Is that what you want to do?   580

GLYKERA
> Dearest friend, just do this favor for me.

PATAIKOS
> It will be done, but it's rash and foolish.
> Don't you see what a move like this will mean?

GLYKERA
> I know best what suits me best.

PATAIKOS
> You'll have your wish. Do any of your slaves
> know the location of this prized possession?

GLYKERA
> Doris does. She'll show you and give it to you.

PATAIKOS *(to a slave standing near)*
>Call Doris out here.
(to Glykera)
>>>>Glykera, listen,
>perhaps the right words—the right sort of truce
>between yourself and Polemon . . .   590

DORIS *(coming outside, distressed)*
>Oh mistress!

GLYKERA
>What has happened?

DORIS
>Something bad.

GLYKERA
>Doris, just bring me that little chest—
>you know the one I mean. What's this about?
>Why are you crying? You know the one, by Zeus!
>The one with the lovely little things inside.
(Doris goes into the house and brings out the little chest. She opens it and
>>>>>*Pataikos stares at the contents in bafflement.)*

PATAIKOS
>By Zeus the savior, I feel very strange.
>Yet nothing is wholly impossible . . .
>These things look familiar, I've seen them before.   600
>Before you unfold the embroidery,
>just tell me, doesn't a goat or a cow
>stand next in this line of little figures?

GLYKERA
>My dear, it's a deer, not a goat.

PATAIKOS *(with mounting excitement)*
>Well, anyway, something with horns.
>And after that comes a horse with wings . . .

I'd know my dear wife's work just anywhere,
that poor, sad woman whom I loved so much.
(*Moschion enters from the right. They don't see each other as Moschion*
mutters to himself in a daze.)

MOSCHION
It's not impossible, it seems to me.
My mother might have had a daughter   610
at the time when she gave birth to me.
If that's true, then she could be my sister.
If *that* is true, I'm ruined, lost, unlucky . . .
(*Moschion stands off to the side, mumbling to himself.*)

PATAIKOS (*looking up at the sky*)
O Zeus! Is it possible that something
is left to me of my lost family?

GLYKERA (*starting to feel agitated herself*)
Ask me now whatever you want to know.

PATAIKOS
Tell me how you came to have these items.

GLYKERA
When I was a baby, I was swaddled
in this embroidery that you see here.

MOSCHION (*overhearing*)
This is no small matter. I am hurled   620
by fate to a critical time in my life.

PATAIKOS (*to Glykera*)
Were you alone when you were found?
Just tell me—that I need to know.

GLYKERA
No. Someone exposed my brother with me.

MOSCHION *(aside)*
> That's one of the things I was asking about!

PATAIKOS
> Then how were you taken, one from the other?

GLYKERA
> I could repeat everything, for I've been told.
> But I'll reveal only my part of the story.
> I swore to her that I'd be silent
> for his sake, about my twin, my brother.   630

MOSCHION *(aside)*
> Now she's given another clear sign—
> She swore to the woman I call mother,
> and now where on earth do I belong?

PATAIKOS *(to Glykera)*
> Who found you then and reared you?

GLYKERA
> The woman who found me lying there,
> she raised me as well as she could.

PATAIKOS
> Did she tell you the place where you were found?

GLYKERA
> She said it was a shaded place—
> also that there was running water near.

PATAIKOS
> That's what he told me—the man who put you there.   640

GLYKERA
> Who was he? If it is right, then tell me.

PATAIKOS
>A slave. But the person who grudged you life—
>I must admit it—that was I.

GLYKERA
>You—my father—put me there! But why?

PATAIKOS
>Many things were unexpected, my child—
>your mother died when she gave birth to you
>and then, it was just a single day before . . .

GLYKERA *(interrupting, excitedly)*
>What happened then? I tremble hearing this.

PATAIKOS
>Used to being comfortable with money,
>I became impoverished in one day.   650

GLYKERA
>In one day! Gods! What a terrible fate.

PATAIKOS
>I heard that my ship, which furnished our wealth,
>had disappeared in the Aegean Sea.

GLYKERA
>And that was a fateful day for me.

PATAIKOS
>I thought that a beggar without a cent
>was a fool to try to bring up children.
>I didn't know what to do with my twins,
>so I had them exposed. Tell me now,
>what else was found there with the two of you?

GLYKERA

    There are things that I was told—necklaces,   660
    and leatherwork, and this embroidery,
    and also a jeweled ornament
    was left behind to identify us.

PATAIKOS

    I'd like to see that jewel very much.

GLYKERA

    I don't have it any more. I assume
    it was left for my brother to have.

MOSCHION *(aside)*

    Can it be? It seems that he's my father!

PATAIKOS

    Could you tell me more about those things?

GLYKERA

    There was a large purple band . . .

PATAIKOS *(excitedly interrupting her)*

    Indeed, there was!   670

GLYKERA

    A line of dancing girls was on it.

MOSCHION *(aside)*

    I think I need no further proof!

GLYKERA

    And also a piece of very sheer cloth,
    and a golden headband was there as well.
    That's all there was.

PATAIKOS

> I don't have the need to hear any more.
> Dearest, my daughter, greet your father.
> (*Pataikos and Glykera hug one another. Moschion now goes up to them*
> *and addresses Pataikos.*)

MOSCHION

> Now I am here, and I'm your long-lost son.
> Let me take part in this embrace as well.

PATAIKOS

> My goodness, who is this young man to me?   680

GLYKERA

> It's true, I knew it, but I couldn't speak,
> afraid to damage his position
> if he were known to be my brother.
> The woman who raised me told me so
> just before she died, to be sure no love
> between us grew inappropriately.
> She wanted me to know I had a brother,
> so I'd have family in case of need.
> Can you just imagine my quandary
> when Moschion ran up and hugged me?   690
> I was too stunned to be touching my brother
> to have the resolve to push him away.

MOSCHION (*soulfully*)

> What you say is true. I rushed up to you,
> really attracted, and never dreaming
> who you might be. I'm sorry now
> for the harm that came your way through me.
> I am the cause of Polemon's rage
> while you did nothing wrong. I'm sorry still
> that I must lose the possibility

of loving you other than as a brother,   700
but am stunned and simply overjoyed
to find my sister and my father here.
I must confess I overheard mother
(that is, the woman I always called mother)
talking to Glykera here, in my house.
That was the first time I ever had learned
that I was adopted by her. She took
a neighbor in need of protection,
and arrogantly I thought she did it
for me. I think I've learned humility.   710
But most of all I have my family!

PATAIKOS *(with his arms around the two of them)*
I have you both now, happiness undreamed
all these years when I was left alone.
Finally I did regain my fortune,
but always felt the pain of loss in my heart.
Now I feel we must resolve the issue
between my Glykera and Polemon.
No one can have everything, but perhaps
we can end these problems happily.
Let us get out of the way now. That band   720
of celebrating youths have come again.
(The Chorus now appears for its final entr'acte performance.)

CHORUS
Deianeira, loving Heracles,
resorted to the Centaur's magic.
With wine, the heart can find a bit of ease.
Desist from acting parts of tragic
dimensions in their inner core.
Drink wine and do not suffer more
the pain of lost and disprized love
which intellect can't rise above.

ACT V

(Doris and Polemon come out of Polemon's house after the chorus leaves. They are deep in conversation.)

DORIS

And so you see, that is how they found out   730
that they are twins, and how Pataikos
is the father that they lost as babies.

POLEMON *(holding his head down miserably)*

Lost. That's the word for me. I lost it all.
Lost my temper and then I lost my love.
Now I have no hold on her at all—
I might as well just go and hang myself.

DORIS

Don't, please don't . . .

POLEMON

But what shall I do, Doris? How can I live?
I'm utterly worthless without her.

DORIS *(consoling)*

Just wait, and she'll return to you.   740

POLEMON

By the Gods, how can that be?

DORIS

You've got to put your mind to it now.
Behave like a civilized sort of man.

POLEMON

There's nothing that I wouldn't do.
Doris, go and tell her now, and hurry!
Tomorrow I will set you free.

How can you talk to someone unwilling?
She's gone! I know she's gone away from me.
Oh, I am conquered by her as a force
of nature or an army overwhelmed.   750
He was her brother, not her lover,
but I got drunk like a jealous madman
and made a mess of everything. Dear me!
Doris, dearest, tell me what to do.

DORIS

    I'll go into the house and speak with her now.
(Doris enters Myrrhine's house, while Polemon paces outside. After a
               little while she comes out and addresses Polemon.)
    You're in luck. She's coming out to you.

POLEMON

    She wasn't just having a laugh at me?

DORIS

    By Aphrodite, no. She was only
    just putting on her robe. Her father
    is still asking questions, wanting to hear more.   760
    First you must show happiness for her.

POLEMON

    By Zeus, you're right. Now I must think of her.
    The cook's inside. He should sacrifice
    the pig in honor of this miracle.

DORIS

    Where's the basket and the other things we need?
    Where's the barley, the garland, and the knife?

POLEMON

    The basket can come later. Slay the pig,
    or rather perhaps I should do it myself.

But first I'll get a garland from an altar,
and then I'll wear it, put it on myself.   770

DORIS

That will make you seem much more convincing.

POLEMON

Can't you just go and ask her
if she means to come out soon?

DORIS

I told you she's coming, and Pataikos
is coming outside with her to you.

POLEMON

Her father himself! I think I can't stand this.
I'm going home. Call me when its over.
(There is a noise at Myrrhine's door.)

DORIS

Wait for me—does the rattling frighten you?
(Doris follows Polemon into his house, trying to calm him down.
Meanwhile, Pataikos and Glykera emerge from
Myrrhine's house, with Moschion following.)

PATAIKOS *(to Glykera)*

I'm happy that you are saying
you can come to some agreement.   780
It shows that you are truly a good Greek.
In your good fortune you settle the case.
(calls to a slave)
Boy, run and call out Polemon now.

POLEMON *(subdued)*

I'm coming out, about to celebrate
Glykera's good luck and Pataikos' too.
I learned she's just found her father in you.

PATAIKOS
>What you heard is right, and now I intend
>to give her today in marriage to you,
>and may you have many legitimate children.

POLEMON *(quickly)*
>I'll take her now . . .   790

PATAIKOS
>I also give three talents as a dowry.

POLEMON *(unable to believe his good luck)*
>That's very kind of you.

PATAIKOS *(sternly)*
>From now on, behave as a soldier.
>Don't forget, and don't be rash in any way.

POLEMON
>By Apollo, I almost died
>a little while ago. *I* won't go headlong
>into anything. I'll never say
>a word against you, Glykera—
>Just forgive me, darling.

PATAIKOS
>This time it happened that your drunken rage   800
>started our good fortunes into motion.

POLEMON
>What you say is true.

PATAIKOS
>Because of this you have your forgiveness.

POLEMON
>Celebrate with us, Pataikos.

PATAIKOS
> Just now I have another task to perform.
> Moschion will marry the daughter of Philinos.
> I'm going to make the arrangements.
> May the Earth prove fruitful for you all.

MOSCHION *(subdued, resigned)*
> Father, I will do as you say. It's time
> for me to settle down. I've found few men   810
> who ever got whatever they wished for.
> Meanwhile, here's to Glykera, my sister,
> and to Polemon, my brother and my friend.
> Father is filling out his family—
> I think we'll have a double wedding soon.

DORIS
> And I will have my freedom, as he said.
> Audience, rejoice! Celebrate with us.

The Girl from Samos (Samia)

Translated by
Richard Elman

Translator's Preface

Texts of this late Greek play exist as shards, tea leaves at best, bits of resinous rosemary, sage, sesame, and lemon blossom, prevailing smells even today on certain Attic streets. They were, in fact, the mere fragments of this play on papyrus, taken chiefly from the wrappings of corpses, though with large ellipses. Either the plays were not so highly thought of in their day, or papyrus was too valuable, and not to be wasted.

Samos signified an isle of abundance to Greeks of Menander's time. The woman referred to in the title is an Athenian's mistress. She nurses his son's baby from her breasts, having lost a child of her own in pregnancy. According to Menander, Samos was such a fertile isle that even the birds gave milk.

Though choruses are indicated in the texts for this play, they have not been recorded in any existing archives. Perhaps they were improvised. Antic bits of Attic *tit arse*, to use the Brit expression. The play, such as it is, does have a rowdy air, like a sitcom. Many of Menander's comic types have survived over time in Plautus, in Comedia dell' Arte, in Shakespeare's comedies, in slapstick movies, on TV: the fresh servant, the self-righteous old gent, the rakish stud hoist, as it were, by his own peter.

I enjoyed playing with this tempest among the neighbors in Athens, and thought of the choruses as both celebratory and deprecating, as in early Brecht-Weil, or perhaps Cole Porter. Most of the action takes place between the stoops of Demeas and Nikeratos, who have just returned from a business trip to the East; and Demeas' "squeeze" must shuttle between the two abjectly. Might this play have been called "She *Shtups* to Conquer"?

Menander wrote in verse, and I've tried to preserve that through occasional rhyming with frequent runovers. Faced with so many ellipses, I've kept to the best guesses of scholars as to the specific details of lost plot and scenic situations. If I've taken some liberties with language and the demotic with this fourth-century B.C. mise en scène, it's to suggest the urban racy tone of such a late Athenian comedy.

When the sons and daughters of solid businessmen and neighbors like Demeas and Nikeratos get into trouble, it's no laughing matter in their neighborhood in their part of town. Or is it? Girls were always getting into trouble like that where I grew up, and everybody on the stoop knew before the parents. How Plangon's belly belied detection for so long is nowhere indicated in the play. Moschion may have put a duck in her oven, but he's shown to be a good lad at heart, though a little weak in the knees. So are they all. Plunge on to Plangon who never even makes an appearance until her marriage is enacted! And enjoy, folks!

Cast

MOSCHION, a young Athenian gentleman
CHRYSIS, a Samian girl, Demeas' mistress
PARMENON, servant to Moschion and Demeas
DEMEAS, Moschion's adoptive father
NIKERATOS, Demeas' neighbor
CHORUS of revelers
COOK
NONSPEAKING
   Servants
   Baby
   Nikeratos' wife
   Plangon, Nikeratos' daughter

*(A street in Athens with two houses left and right and, in the center,
an image of Apollo and altar to the God.)*

ACT I

*(Moschion, a young man of rakish good looks, paces back and forth
between the two porches while addressing the audience.)*

MOSCHION
   Foundlings have
   the luck of starfish.
   I'm all washed up now
   like a soap dish.
   Demeas adopted me
   when I was just
   a little calf,
   so now I give him
   back dishonor
   with a shaft!   10
(turning left)

This fine house is his, where I once scampered,
(turning right)
    and this the house of Nikeratos, family friend,
    in which his child, a former virgin of the place,
    without his knowledge is bestowed as damaged goods.

How I was pampered here
Apollo knows! I desired
Nikeratos' daughter. But when
my father and his friend
went off together on business
my desire mixed with hers,   20
and to our mutual shame
there is a child.
Must I tell you all the details?

On calm seas of domesticity
the foundling child is apt to founder.
What's the point of my pretending I'm not to blame?

When the maidenhead has vanished,
morality is blemished. About this I feel helpless.
It hurts me, since I know I really wronged
the girl, Plangon, by loving her,   30
and I wronged Nikeratos as well.

Telling my own story will be
painful, but you'll get to see
how generous Demeas can be.

Right from the start,
when I was hardly even a boy,
I got every kind of toy.

When I was so young
I could not read the stars above,
he offered me a father's love.   40

Nobody was allowed
to treat me any differently
from any other heir apparent.

Garbed in fine linen, I was one
of our crowd, as the saying goes,
though rags had been my swaddling clothes.

At Demeas' expense I had success
in the theater, was a dashing
officer of the Guards with fine

horses, a man of fashion,   50
gave money to charity and
to friends in need, never once

stepping out of line until
father and Chrysis got together.
When I found out he was connected

to a Samian girl, Demeas
turned a little bashful and embarrassed
about his new passion,

until I convinced him to bring her
into our house as her protector   60
and keep the younger rivals out.

This he did, but when she got
pregnant and he was going off

with Nikeratos, Demeas told
her to abort the child, and she
would not, and trouble got the better of me.
Plangon's mother was close to Chrysis,
and used to visit at our house often

with her daughter. One day I came home
from the farm and found them all here   70
celebrating the feast of Adonis

on the roof of the house with
fresh green garden trays, and noise,
and food, and wine. I must admit

it was an orgiastic scene
for women stashed so high and dry,
always out of the public eye.

Well, as I say, things happened
between the two of us, and, as you know
the result was a baby. Meanwhile Chrysis,   80

having lost that baby of her own
while Demeas was away, took this one
in our house to nurse. I promised

I would marry Plangon as soon as
both fathers returned, but, frankly,
once her lock turned by my key

she seemed of much less value to me.
I'm sad and frightened and confused
at this moment, really not enthused . . .
(He shows alarm and exits left as though in a hurry as he sees Chrysis
approaching with the baby in her arms.)

CHRYSIS
    Although intended for another,   90
    little one, let my milk enrich you.
    Suck sweetly and well.
(hears conversation)

Here comes two people, in a hurry.
I'll hide here and listen
to what they have to say.
(Enter Moschion and Parmenon talking.)

MOSCHION
  You actually saw my father in the harbor?

PARMENON
  How many times must I say it? He's
  back home again with your neighbor.

MOSCHION *(grimly)*
  I'm so pleased.

PARMENON
  Now you've got to be a man,   100
  and tell them of your wish
  to marry Plangon.

MOSCHION
  Now that push has come to shove,
  I've lost my nerve.

PARMENON
  What are you saying?

MOSCHION
  I'm too embarrassed.

PARMENON
  Push came to shove and she
  produced his child when
  he seduced her. Now he's embarrassed?
  What about her? And her mother?   110
  You look sick to your stomach . . .

CHRYSIS *(coming from behind)*
> What's all this scolding I hear?

PARMENON
> You're here too, Chrysis? You
> really want to know what's going on?
> I'd like to see him get his duties done.
> He promised he would marry Plangon.
> He promised garlands, feasting.
> But all he does is mewl outside her door.
> I want the wedding to begin.

> I want him to recall he gave his word.   120
> There should be offerings
> and a wedding cake of pounded sesame,
> and that's my job as servant.
> That's why I'm scolding him—so
> that my marriage tasks can begin.

MOSCHION
> I'll do it. Please don't carry on.

CHRYSIS
> I'm sure you will.

MOSCHION
> What about our baby? Shall we continue
> to pretend he's yours?

CHRYSIS
> Why not?   130

MOSCHION
> Demeas will be angry.

CHRYSIS

>For a little while, but then he'll
>stop. The man's in love, as you are,
>also. Love makes even angry men
>behave themselves with women, given time.
>For the baby, I'd suffer Demeas' rage
>before I let some wetnurse
>suckle him in some Athenian slum.
>Parmenon, prepare. Let's go inside.

(They exit.)

MOSCHION

>That I'm unfeeling and a heel   140
>means I don't know how others feel.
>
>I'm callow, I lack experience
>and am afraid of talking nonsense.
>
>Maybe I should go put a noose
>around my neck? I'm such a wretch.
>
>To think I can plead my own case
>and avoid personal disgrace
>is unduly optimistic. I'll go off
>elsewhere and practice
>my penitence shtick.   150

(He exits. Enter Demeas and Nikeratos with traveling bags and servants.)

DEMEAS

>Don't you see the difference already
>between our home town and that sewer
>where we just were?

NIKERATOS

>Of course. The Black Sea is full of fish
>and sly old men. Byzantium is truly

sickening. It stinks, as bitter as gall.
God! This place delights my soul.

DEMEAS
We wish you, Athens, all deserved
blessings, so we who live here may
be happy and prosper.   160
(to servants)
Take that stuff inside the house.
You there. Are you paralyzed?
(Servants go inside the house.)

NIKERATOS
The most oppressive thing about Byzantium
was not to see the sun for weeks on end,
and fog as sticky as mastic gum.

DEMEAS
What's to see in such a place?
The natives know there's nothing marvelous,
so they get by with just a little daylight.

NIKERATOS
How true.

DEMEAS
That's not our concern. A propos of what   170
we were talking about . . .

NIKERATOS
You mean, of course, Moschion's marriage?

DEMEAS
Exactly.

NIKERATOS
>My mind's made up. Let's pick a date
>and get things underway,
>and good luck to all of us.

DEMEAS
>You've thought this over?

NIKERATOS
>Of course!

DEMEAS
>I agree, and thought so all along.

NIKERATOS
>Drop by after you've unpacked.   180
(He goes inside his house.)

DEMEAS *(self-absorbed)*
>There are still some minor points to settle.
(He looks up and glances about, realizes he's alone. Starts for the house
>*when some revelers appear. There follows a choral*
>*interlude with the revelers as chorus and Demeas*
>*look on.)*

CHORUS

>*Strophe*

>Leda was raped by a swan,
>Europa filled by a bull,
>but a maid and a man
>prove again and again
>the wonderful sexual dance.

Antistrophe

Come, hymen, come!
The groom has pretty legs.
The bride is in disgrace
though not her lovely face.   190
Come, hymen, come!
Though women often act like sheep
parts of them are rather deep.

Strophe

The words of a man to a maid
are often as not betrayed,
and only old Zeus
has a godly excuse
when he lies next to you in the shade.

Antistrophe

Come, hymen, come.
Our revels are begun.   200
Come, hymen, come.
Let's commence the fun.
Chrysis had a son.
But who can be the father?
Riddle me this one!
Come, hymen, come . . .

ACT II

(*Moschion enters from left and Demeas comes out of his house onto
the steps of his porch. They do not see each other at first.*)

MOSCHION

Rehearsing didn't help. When I found a quiet
field outside the city for my peroration, I started imagining
things like wedding ceremonies and the cutting
of the cake, the ladies at the ritual bath   210
in my escort, and processions and gifts and—help!

Here comes Demeas.
He must have heard me. Welcome home, father.

DEMEAS

Glad to see you, son.

MOSCHION

You're looking rather . . . solemn.

DEMEAS

Preoccupied.
I left here thinking I had a mistress,
but I've returned to find I have a wife.

MOSCHION

Married? I don't follow you.

DEMEAS

Without my knowledge or consent I seem   220
to have acquired an infant son.
That baggage can pack him up and
get out of my house. Go to hell
for all I care.

MOSCHION

No, father.

DEMEAS

Why not?
I won't bring a bastard into this house.
I'm not in the mood
to humor a disobedient mistress.

MOSCHION

You're joking. Why should it matter?   230
Legitimate or illegitimate? To love is only human.

DEMEAS
>   Now you must be joking.

MOSCHION
>   I'm really not. What does birth have to do with it?
>   A good man is legitimate; a bad
>   one is a bastard through and through;
>   and she who was passion's slave
>   might also be love's emissary.

DEMEAS
>   Fancy language for unfaithfulness.

MOSCHION
>   You don't know that, father.
>   That child could have been conceived before your departure.   240

DEMEAS
>   And so it was, but I demanded that she do
>   something to rid herself . . .

MOSCHION
>   Of love? O father, think of that.
>   You surely matter to her that she
>   plants your seed in our front garden.
>   Now you would reject the fruit?

DEMEAS *(remorseful)*
>   Even so . . . but I'm not sure.

MOSCHION
>   Better to take no chances, wait and see.

DEMEAS
>   Oh, sure . . . and you? What will you do
>   to bring me heirs? Nikeratos says   250
>   you can marry Plangon any time.

MOSCHION

> Then, of course, I will. I mean . . .
> I'm longing to be married, father,
> and to be obedient, not just seem so.

DEMEAS

> Good lad! You shall marry her at once
> if our neighbors are ready.

MOSCHION

> I'm serious. No need to question that.

DEMEAS

> Ask no questions? You're serious?
> Right, son. I'll run straight over
> to our neighbors and tell them to get   260
> ready for the wedding. Everything from
> our households will be prepared for you.

MOSCHION

> Now I'll ready myself, and pour a libation,
> and sprinkle myself with holy water,
> burn some incense—and then I'll go
> and fetch my Plangon home to me.

DEMEAS

> Hold off a moment longer till we have
> her father's actual consent.

MOSCHION

> He can't say no. But I shall wait outside,
> so as not to interfere with what they shall prepare.   270

DEMEAS

> I had no idea that Moschion was so in love.
> Coincidences like this are the work of a divinity,

always looking after the things we cannot see.
Moschion is head over heels and can hardly wait.
(He sees Nikeratos coming out of his house and calls out to him.)
     Hey there, Nikeratos.
(His neighbor stands on his porch.)

NIKERATOS
     What now, friend?

DEMEAS
     The children are hot to trot.

NIKERATOS
     Meaning what, may I ask you?

DEMEAS
     We must have a wedding this very day.
     The preparations are already underway.   280
     Here's Parmenon. Hey, Parmenon . . .

PARMENON *(from the house)*
     Yes, master . . .

DEMEAS
     Go and fetch garlands, an animal to sacrifice,
     sesame seeds for a cake. Empty out the marketplace
     and come back here straight away.

PARMENON
     You're leaving that to me, sir?

DEMEAS
     And hurry! Right away.
     And bring us back a cook.

PARMENON
     A cook? After I've bought all the rest?

DEMEAS
　　Exactly.   290

PARMENON
　　I'll take some money and you'll see my back.
　　(He goes back inside the house.)

DEMEAS
　　Have you been to the market yet, Nikeratos?

NIKERATOS
　　Let me tell my wife first. Then I'm on
　　my way, right after Parmenon.

PARMENON *(comes out of house with a basket, hurrying)*
　　I wish I knew exactly what was coming off,
　　but I am off and hurrying anyway,
　　as you've ordered me to do, master.

DEMEAS
　　Nikeratos will have to persuade his wife
　　not to raise a fuss. Who has time for
　　explanations? What? You're still here, Parmenon?   300
　　Off with you. Be quick . . . Run, man!
(Nikeratos enters his house, Parmenon scampers off stage, Demeas stands
alone as the Chorus of revelers reenters.)

DEMEAS
　　Great Dionysus knows, there's
　　nothing like a proper wedding
　　celebration with everybody
　　letting down their hair.
　　This festive time is
　　something we can share.

CHORUS

Strophe

When a daughter's and a son's
sacred nuptials have begun,
memories will disinter   310
gay affairs from yesteryear:

How priapic was the groom!
How ecstatic was the bride!
How often did he wield his broom
to lift her on his magic ride!

Antistrophe

Wonderful the drunken revel
when the relatives dishevel
and the wedding party bleats
like a goat with swollen teats.

And old marriages reach a boil   320
from the sweaty sullen toil
of this Attic celebration
and the guests' inebriation.

Strophe

And the rhythm and the prance
of the bridegroom's wedding dance,
and the relatives talk dirt
when his manhood lifts his skirt.

And the bride no longer maid
dances on these fertile grounds,
and the bedboards wildly shaking   330
mute the dancers' raucous sounds.

ACT III

(Demeas appears from his house.)

DEMEAS

On long voyages storms suddenly boil up and
capsize the voyager in his boat. You're running
with the wind and all is yaw, and then suddenly
you're over your head in fierce waves and can hardly find a
       breath.
That's what just happened to me inside the house.
I was smoothly getting ready for the celebration just
five minutes ago, making sure the spirit and
the flesh would each be given their due, when
splash, I got it right in the face.   340

(He starts downstage to address the audience directly.)

I want to tell you all personally I've been scuttled,
the victim of a domestic disaster. Am I sane
or mad? I simply don't know what to believe.
Maybe I'm getting the facts all wrong and bringing this on
       myself.
In the house I went about my tasks expeditiously,
giving the servants straightforward orders
for everything—the cleaning up, the baking,
the barley, the garlic, the knife for the
ritual sacrifice. And it all was coming off
nicely, but we were all so rushed there was   350
a certain amount of confusion. The infant
was stashed on a couch, away from all the
rest of us, and he was howling mad for
being neglected. The women servants were
shouting at each other: "Flour! Water!
Please, somebody, oil! Anybody got the charcoal?"
And I was lending them a hand, passing along
this and that, when I happened to enter the
pantry. I had to check on the supplies. While

I was in there a woman came downstairs and   360
went into the room next door where the weaving gets done
(to enter the pantry you go through that room).
And she was Moschion's old nurse, who is really
getting on now. Once she'd been a slave of
mine, but long ago I set her free. When she
heard the baby crying, and none to look
after it, she went and picked him up
and coddled him, cooing at him in baby
talk: "There now sweet pie . . . what a little
love. Where's mummy's precious boy?" She   370
walked him up and down and coddled him,
and when his crying ceased I heard her
whisper to herself, "It seems only yesterday
that I was looking after Moschion like
this, and now I'm coddling his son . . ."

It's not funny. Imagine how I felt.
A servant girl came rushing in just then,
and the nurse, she said, "Why not give
the baby his bath? Why wait? It's his
father's wedding day. You shouldn't be neglecting him."   380
"Master's at home. Don't shout," the girl said.
"That can't be," the old crone said.
"Where is he?"
"Next door in the pantry!"
And then with her voice raised:
"Be quick! Mistress needs you, Nurse," and under her breath,
"He hasn't even heard a word! We're lucky."
"Me and my tongue," the old one said,
and off she went I wish I knew where.
Quite calmly, I walked out of there   390
as though I hadn't heard a thing, just
as I tried to do here a moment ago.
But in the outer room I saw my woman,
Chrysis, with the infant, nursing him,

and when I saw those lovely breasts like that
I knew she was, of course, the child's
real mother. But who was the father? Me?
Ladies and gentlemen, I still can't
bring myself to say what I think I heard
and what I think I know. I'm not angry   400
right now, not yet. I know the lad, he's
a good lad, and has always behaved very
properly toward me. But then I remember
the old woman was once Moschion's nurse,
and what she said, not knowing I was
listening, and when I look at Chrysis
and how she obviously adores this child,
and has insisted against my wishes on
keeping it—Well I may not be angry,
but I am out of my mind with jealousy.   410

Oh good! Here's my man Parmenon,
back from the market with his people.
I'll let him stow them in the house.
(Parmenon enters with provisions, a cook, and other servants.)

PARMENON
A cook like you who carries about a sharp knife
is really quite capable of
cutting all of us up into little pieces
with your tongue. For God's sakes, man . . .

COOK *(with hauteur)*
How could you ever understand? You're not an artist.

PARMENON
Really?

COOK
Certainly not to me, you aren't. I was   420
only asking for some facts: the number

of guests, how many ladies will be eating,
the hour we serve, and if we need an extra waiter.
Is the dinner service big enough?
Is the kitchen protected from the elements?
Will everything I need be available?

PARMENON
   I think you're already cooking my carcass, maestro.

COOK
   Go boil your head in rosemary and thyme.

PARMENON
   The same to you with a barrel of live eels,
   and make a good job of it.   430
(to the cook and the other servants)
   Inside now, all of you, and get busy.
(Cook and others enter the house.)

DEMEAS
   Parmenon?

PARMENON
   Am I being summoned?

DEMEAS
   It's me, and you are.

PARMENON
   Oh?
(slightly bewildered)
   It's only you, sir.

DEMEAS
   Enough of that! Bring your basket to the ladies and
   come right back here.

PARMENON
   Yes sir!
(He swaggers inside.)

DEMEAS
   Nothing in my house escapes this knave.
   He has his finger in every nook.   440
   But here he comes again.
(Parmenon is talking into the house as he backs out again.)

PARMENON
   Chrysis, see that the cook lacks nothing
   he needs, and keep that old crone the
   nurse away from the wine jugs.
(He almost bumps into Demeas and spins around.)
   At your service, sir!

DEMEAS
   Indeed, my service.
(grimly)
   Come over here with me, away from that door.

PARMENON
   Here I am!

DEMEAS
   Let's get this straight. I'm not out to
   beat you. I want to clear some things up.   450

PARMENON
   Beat me? Why whatever for?

DEMEAS
   I've just discovered you're part of a
   conspiracy to keep something from me.

PARMENON

Me, sir? I swear by everything sacred
and all the hosts of Heaven . . .

DEMEAS

No more of that! I'm not guessing. I know.

PARMENON

May the gods strike me dead . . .

DEMEAS

Look me in the eye, man to man.

PARMENON

I'm looking.

DEMEAS

That baby—whose is it?   460

PARMENON

Er, well . . .

DEMEAS

I want an answer!

PARMENON

Chrysis'?

DEMEAS

And the father?

PARMENON

According to her, you are, sir.

DEMEAS

Now you've done it. You're lying at my expense.

PARMENON

    Me sir? It's certainly not mine.
    Sincerely, I can swear to you.

DEMEAS

    Stop this foolishness. I know the
    whole story. Every last detail.   470
    I've heard tell it's Moschion's child,
    that you're in on this scam, and
    that she's nursing him for Moschion's sake.

PARMENON

    Who would ever say such a thing?

DEMEAS

    Answer me. Is it true?

PARMENON

    In a manner of speaking, I suppose.
    But we didn't want it known.

DEMEAS *(outraged)*

    Not want it known by me! Bring me
    a horsewhip, someone. I need to deal
    with this viper I've been harboring!   480

PARMENON

    Oh, please, sir, no!

DEMEAS

    I'll flog you and brand you alive.

PARMENON

    Brand me?

DEMEAS

    Right now!

PARMENON
    Help! I've had it!
(He starts to flee.)

DEMEAS
    Come back here! Where are you going?
    I've got some proper medicine for you.
    Grab him, someone!
(raising hands to heaven)
    O Gods, O Heaven on high, help me!
(stops and glances about)
    Why all the noisy imprecation, Demeas?   490
    Why all the shouting? Control yourself,
    you damn fool. Control!
    It wasn't Moschion who put horns on your head.
(to the audience)
    That may seem a bit far-fetched,
    ladies and gentlemen, I know, but it's true.
    If he'd done this out of malice, or in the
    throes of passion, or from dislike of me,
    he'd be boasting all over town, and seeking the support
    of others. Making fun of the old goat!
    But he showed he was not so taken with   500
    her, in my judgment, by agreeing to
    marry Plangon right away. He wants to
    get away from this house of sin, and from
    that Helen who was once my mistress.
    For what's happened, she's the only one
    I blame. She seduced him when he was in
    his cups, or randy as a hare, not able to
    exercise self-restraint. That's what happened
    here, obviously. Samian wine and a young
    man's cullions can work a lot of mischief   510
    when he finds beside him someone eager
    to set snares for him. I refuse to believe
    that this boy, who always was appreciative

of my goodness to him, would do this to me
deliberately. Not even were he ten times
adopted and not a child of blood. It's his
character I want to stress, not his ancestors.
But that Samian girl . . . that witch . . . she's
a whore. Pure poison . . . and she'll have to leave.

Be a man, Demeas. Never mind how you   520
missed her all this time. For your son's
sake pretend nothing untoward happened, and throw
that bitch out on her ear. Return her to
the streets. Let her swing a purse to
get by. You have a perfect alibi. Say
that she kept the child against your
wishes. Nothing more.
      Honor of the family!
(*Enter Cook from house.*)

COOK
      Hey, Parmenon! Where are you?
(*shouts*)
      Damn him! Running out on me without   530
      even lifting a finger to help me.

DEMEAS (*rushing toward the house*)
      Out of my way, damn you!

COOK
      What's this? Some gray-haired lunatic
      just ran into the house? What's happening?
      Nothing to do with me, I hope. Can't be.
      He's a nut, shouting at me at the top of his voice.
      He could shatter all my place settings.
      Curses on that Parmenon for bringing me
      to this madhouse. What's this? What's happening now?
(*He steps to one side of the door as Demeas pushes Chrysis with her baby
                    out of the house.*)

DEMEAS
You heard me—get out!   540

CHRYSIS
Where shall we go?

DEMEAS
Go to hell, for all I care.

CHRYSIS
Pity me.

DEMEAS
Pity you? Your tears don't move me.
But a kick in the ass will move you!
No more games!

CHRYSIS
Games? What games?

DEMEAS *(still wishing to keep the scandal a secret)*
I'll say no more. You've got the
infant, and the old woman.
Now go swing a purse!   550

CHRYSIS
Is it because I kept the baby?

DEMEAS
Yes, and . . .

CHRYSIS
What?

DEMEAS
That's bad enough.

COOK *(aside)*
>So that's the story. Now I see.

DEMEAS
>You had it real good with me and you didn't even know it.

CHRYSIS
>Please! I'm not following you at all.

DEMEAS
>You came to me in just a little cotton dress.
>That was all you owned, and . . .

CHRYSIS
>So?   560

DEMEAS
>When you were threadbare, I could do no wrong by you.

CHRYSIS
>That's still the case.

DEMEAS
>Don't act like that! You have everything I
>ever gave you. I'll let you have some servants
>too. Now leave.

COOK *(aside)*
>Here's a fine frenzy, a regular fricazee. I've got enough
>on my hands without this.
>*(walks toward Demeas)*
>Sir? Look here.

DEMEAS
>Mind your own business!

COOK
>No need to shout and snap!   570

DEMEAS *(ignoring him)*
>Another woman would have been thrilled with
>all I had to offer her, and never give
>my love a sideways glance.

COOK
>What's he getting at now?

DEMEAS
>You're taking your son, and all that's yours. Go!
>And take what you want!

COOK *(aside)*
>She still doesn't get it.
>*(to Demeas)*
>Nevertheless, sir . . .

DEMEAS
>I'll knock your teeth out if you speak a word.

COOK
>This isn't a celebration, it's a potential massacre.   580
>I'm getting out of here.
>*(He goes back inside the house.)*

DEMEAS *(heartbroken)*
>Once you're on your own, Chrysis,
>you'll be just like all the other women
>of the town, a party girl for rent
>and pleasure. You'll be fed and fondled
>and drink too much, and die. Those
>who can't do this just starve . . . but
>you . . . you won't starve. You'll do
>it smartly until you're old and lose

your looks. Then you'll have learned   590
the hard way what a stupid mistake you
made by double-crossing me.
(She moves toward him.)
    Stay where you are! I can't . . .
(He rushes toward the house.)

CHRYSIS
    Now what shall I do? What's to become of me?
(Enter Nikeratos from the market leading a sheep.)

NIKERATOS
    This fine lamb, when it is gutted, will
    sate all the inhabitants of Heaven for rituals.
    The blood, the gall bladder, the bones,
    the enlarged spleen—such things are craved
    by the Olympians. I'll make a grackle of the
    skin and send the tasty bits to friends: 600
    and a little for me and my wife. What
    do I see here?
(seeing Chrysis with the baby in her arms and tears on her face)
    Chrysis crying in the street? What could be happening?

CHRYSIS
    Your dear old friend has thrown me out.

NIKERATOS
    Demeas? Why?

CHRYSIS
    Because of the baby.

NIKERATOS
    I heard from my womenfolk that you'd kept
    the child and were nursing him, which was
    perhaps a foolish thing to do with Demeas,
    but I know my friend. He's a good chap.   610

He'll calm down eventually. Was he
angry right from the start? Or only after a while?

CHRYSIS

At first he seemed fine, told me to get
the house ready for the wedding, and
then, when I had my fill of chores, burst
in on me like an ogre, and dragged me from
the house and locked the doors.

NIKERATOS

Clearly his mind has gone blotto. The Black Sea is
not a healthy climate. Come along, dear,
and see my wife. She'll look after you   620
and cheer you up. And then Demeas will
come to his senses and everything will
be all right once again after he thinks
about what he's done.

(He leads Chrysis and the baby into the house with him. The stage is
                    empty, and from the distance we hear the Chorus
                    of Revelers approaching.)

CHORUS

Graybeards who sleep with young women
are often of the opinion
that someone else is peeling her onion
and has gotten right down to the core.

(They appear on stage.)

When they go away on a trip, their fears
back home in the master's bedroom creep   630
between the master's sheets, like a whore,
between the master's bedroom sheets.

What lovely interludes are forgotten,
when he imagines others in his place,
prone with her, and face to face,
naked with her, and face to face.

We Greeks have a word for this:
to take a bull by his horns.
How we despoil every tenderness
with the horns we implant on our heads.   640
(*They start off stage in the other direction.*)
Men think that women are easy to get
and women want only their stamina,
but a woman's heart is so intricate
you'd need oracles just to examine her.
(*Song fades out.*)

ACT IV

(*Enter Nikeratos, backing out of his house as he speaks to his wife.*)

NIKERATOS
Woman, you're driving me crazy with your pestering.
I'm off to speak to him now.
(*He turns about to face Demeas' house as the door shuts.*)
I'd have given much of my fortune to prevent this.
By Zeus I would! In the middle of our
wedding preparations this unpleasantness has
upset everybody. Chrysis has sought sanctuary with us   650
all in tears, and the women of my household
are very upset and in tears themselves.
To just throw her out with a child in her arms?
Demeas must be a bully, and I'll see he pays for this.
(*Enter Moschion left without seeing Nikeratos.*)

MOSCHION
Will it be afternoon forever? Will the sun never set?
How long must I wait until we all get started?
I'll go and take another soothing bath, my third for this day.

NIKERATOS
Glad to see you, Moschion.

MOSCHION
> Is the wedding getting underway?
> I just saw Parmenon in the market, and that's   660
> what he said. Shall I fetch your daughter?

NIKERATOS
> You have no idea what's been going on?

MOSCHION
> No.

NIKERATOS
> Miseries galore. Don't even ask me.

MOSCHION
> I haven't heard a thing. What can it be?

NIKERATOS
> Your father has just given Chrysis
> the door. He's thrown her out of his house.

MOSCHION
> Whatever for? You can't be serious.

NIKERATOS
> That's the miserable truth.

MOSCHION
> But why?   670

NIKERATOS
> The baby . . . because of her baby.

MOSCHION
> Where did she go?

NIKERATOS
    She's with us now.

MOSCHION
    What an awful thing to do. It's so unlike him.

NIKERATOS
    You think so too. Then . . .
(He comes up and starts whispering in Moschion's ear as Demeas leaves
                his house while speaking to those inside.)

DEMEAS
    If I had a stick, I'd knock all of your heads
    until you cried. Stop all this nonsense!
    Go and help the cook.
(with sarcasm)
    I must say, that's something to cry over.
    Our house has lost such a valuable bauble?   680
    That Samian's behavior makes duplicity all too clear.
(sees the altar and bows)
    Enable us to celebrate
    a happy marriage,
(turning to the audience)
    for celebrate it I shall, ladies and gentlemen,
    and keep my rage to myself.
(back to altar)
    Protect me, Lord Apollo, from duplicity, so
    I may sing the marriage hymn wholeheartedly.
(with gloom)
    I'll probably not be in very good
    voice, in my present state.
    What of it?   690
    Who cares now?

NIKERATOS
    Try to reason with him, boy. You first.

MOSCHION

 Very well.
(comes forward)
 Father, why are you being this way?

DEMEAS

 What way, son?

MOSCHION

 Must I explain? Why have Chrysis and the baby
 left our house? Tell me please.

DEMEAS *(aside)*

 Someone is being diplomatic. Oh, my . . .
(to Moschion)
 This is none of your business, frankly.
(aside)
 I think he's part of this plot against me. Dreadful . . .   700

MOSCHION

 Begging your pardon . . .

DEMEAS *(aside)*

 It must be he is one of them, or
 why come and speak for her? He should
 be pleased by what I've done . . . from the
 point of view of brazen self-interest . . .

MOSCHION

 What do you think your friends will say when
 they hear about all this?

DEMEAS

 You leave my friends out of this, son. I'll
 take care of them . . .

MOSCHION

    I'd be lacking in breeding if I didn't try to stop you.   710

DEMEAS

    Just you try.

MOSCHION

    Yes I will.

DEMEAS

    This takes the cake. It's even more scandalous
    than I'd imagined.

MOSCHION

    You can't just let your anger get the better of you.

NIKERATOS *(approaching)*

    He's right, Demeas.

MOSCHION

    Nikeratos, go inside and find Chrysis, and have
    her come out here at once.

DEMEAS

    Never mind that! Never mind. For the third time,
    I'm telling you I know everything.   720

MOSCHION

    Everything? What do you mean?

DEMEAS

    Don't mince words with me, son.

MOSCHION

    For your own sake I have to, father.

DEMEAS

> You'll do no such thing. Am I not the master
> of this house?

MOSCHION

> Do it for me, as a favor!

DEMEAS

> A favor? Quit this place and leave you two
> together? If you've any sense at all, you'll
> get on with your wedding arrangements.

MOSCHION

> Yes, of course. But I'd like Chrysis to be   730
> one of the witnesses.

DEMEAS

> You want Chrysis, too.

MOSCHION

> Of course I do, mainly for your sake.

DEMEAS *(aside)*

> Now I know he's one of them, my own
> son. Let Heaven witness: My own son has
> joined with my enemies and is plotting against
> me. I could burst a blood vessel. I really could . . .

MOSCHION

> What are you talking about now?

DEMEAS

> You really can't guess?

MOSCHION

> Of course not.   740

DEMEAS *(whispering)*
>   Come closer. I'll tell you.

MOSCHION *(closer)*
>   Tell me . . .

DEMEAS
>   As you wish! The child is yours. I know.
>   Parmenon told me who is your confidant.
>   So don't pretend . . .

MOSCHION
>   I won't deny it. What harm is Chrysis
>   doing since the child is mine?

DEMEAS
>   Who else is to blame? Tell me that . . .

MOSCHION
>   How is she at fault?

DEMEAS
>   Have you two no shame? No scruples?   750

MOSCHION
>   Why are you shouting at me?

DEMEAS
>   YOU SHIT! I'LL SHOUT! What a foolish
>   thing to say! You're my son. If you take
>   the blame on yourself, how dare you look
>   me in the face and ask me this? Have
>   you no concern for me?

MOSCHION
>   You? Against me? What's going on?

DEMEAS
> Need you ask me?

MOSCHION
> Father, what I did isn't so terrible. Many young
> men have done the same . . .   760

DEMEAS
> God in Heaven. What brass! Face the audience
> and let me ask you: Who is this baby's mother?
> If you don't think it's such a terrible shame,
> tell my friend Nikeratos here . . .

MOSCHION *(aside)*
> If I tell him I'll get my head handed
> to me. Nikeratos will be furious.

NIKERATOS *(joining in)*
> Monster, I'm beginning to see
> it all clearly. This is an outrage.

MOSCHION *(misunderstanding him)*
> Now I've had it!

DEMEAS
> So now you see, Nikeratos?   770

NIKERATOS
> I most certainly do.
> *(in a bemoaning voice)*
> Most awful deed. O Tereus, Oedipus, Thyestes . . .
> All you incestuous loves of legendary times . . .
> you've all been overshadowed by this lad . . .

MOSCHION *(confused)*
> Me?

NIKERATOS

>Such audacity . . . such an insult to the family.
>Demeas, you must assume Amyntor's rage
>and blind your son.

DEMEAS *(to Moschion)*

>It's all because of you he got
>to know of this.   780

NIKERATOS *(still going on about it)*

>Nothing is sacred. No one inviolate! You, the man
>to whom I would have given my daughter
>in marriage, are a monster. I'd rather she wed
>the worst Lothario. I'm not exaggerating.

DEMEAS *(to Moschion)*

>Even though you did me great wrong,
>I tried to keep it quiet.

NIKERATOS

>Don't be weak and cowardly, Demeas. If
>he'd defiled my bed he certainly wouldn't
>be defiling any others. As for his partner,
>that slut, I'd be selling her in the marketplace   790
>the very next day. Then I'd disinherit this
>lout, publicly. In the barbershop or the
>public gardens everybody would know what
>I'd done by first light, and they would
>say, "Nikeratos is no weakling. He means
>what he says about murder, and he's no fool!"

MOSCHION

>What murder? What are you talking about?

NIKERATOS

>When you act against the authority of
>a loving parent, it's murder for sure.

MOSCHION
I'm scared. My throat's so dry I can hardly speak.   800

NIKERATOS
What makes it even worse is I've welcomed
to my humble home the woman responsible
for these outrages.

DEMEAS
Give her the gate, friend, just as I did.
Consider yourself wronged, as a friend
should, when I have been so wronged.

NIKERATOS
I will, with an outburst of indignation
and rage. At just the sight of her I'll
toss that baggage into the streets again.
(to Moschion)
As for you, you savage, dare   810
you look me in the eyes? Out of my way!
(He rushes back inside his house.)

MOSCHION
Father, listen to me now, for God's sake.

DEMEAS
Not a word more!

MOSCHION
I'm just beginning to see it all . . . Nothing
you suspect is true.

DEMEAS
How can that be? Nothing? There's the baby.

MOSCHION

But Chrysis isn't the mother. She's just
protecting me by saying it's hers.

DEMEAS

How? What?

MOSCHION

It's true.   820

DEMEAS

Who belongs to who?
Why is she doing this for you?

MOSCHION

I really don't want you to know, but if you do,
I'll be clear of the charge of offending you
and admit to something much less serious.

DEMEAS

Get on with it! This stalling will be my death.

MOSCHION

The baby's mother is Plangon, Nikeratos' daughter.
I am the father. I was trying to keep all this from you.

DEMEAS

What are you telling me now?

MOSCHION

Only the truth.   830

DEMEAS

Don't bamboozle me! Be careful!

MOSCHION
You can check the facts? Why would I lie about this?

DEMEAS *(thoughtfully)*
I suppose . . .
(startled)
There's the door!
(Nikeratos staggers out of his house.)

NIKERATOS
Oh, miserable. What a sight I've seen.
In a frenzy, I've rushed away,
in pain I had not looked for.

DEMEAS
What the devil is going on now?

NIKERATOS
My only daughter—Plangon—
I came upon her just now breast-feeding his baby.

DEMEAS *(to Moschion)*
That means your story's no lie.   840

MOSCHION
Are you listening, father?

DEMEAS
You didn't wrong me, son, but I wronged you
by suspecting such baseness.

NIKERATOS
I need to have a word with you, Demeas.

MOSCHION
I'm getting out of here.

DEMEAS
>Don't let him scare you!

MOSCHION
>Just to look at him has me frightened to death.
>*(He runs away left.)*

DEMEAS
>Friend, what on earth is wrong?

NIKERATOS
>Breast-feeding the baby in our house is how
>I've just found my only daughter.

DEMEAS
>Maybe she was just pretending.   850

NIKERATOS
>When she saw me she fainted. That was no pretense.

DEMEAS
>Maybe she . . .

NIKERATOS
>Your suppositions will drive me crazy.

DEMEAS *(aside)*
>This is my fault.

NIKERATOS
>Excuse me?

DEMEAS
>I find your story hard to believe.

NIKERATOS
>With my own eyes I saw it.

DEMEAS
> You're babbling.

NIKERATOS
> This is no fairy tale. But I'll go look again.
> *(He starts toward the house once more.)*

DEMEAS
> Hold it right there, friend. I've got an idea.   860
(Nikeratos goes inside.)
> That ruins it. That really messes up everything.
> When he finds out the whole truth he'll
> be in a total rage. Shouting loud
> enough to be heard in Byzantium.
> Nikeratos is a tough guy, coarse,
> insensitive, blunt. This is all
> my fault. My suspicions may bring
> about Moschion's murder. I'm the
> guilty one. I deserve to die. Really!
(Shouts from within Nikeratos' house.)
> What a tumult! He's threatening everybody.   870
> Says he'll burn the baby in his own
> house. I can't stand here and watch
> my grandson roasting. There he is at
> the door again. The man's a natural disaster, a tornado . . .

NIKERATOS *(rushing out)*
> Demeas, Chrysis is plotting
> against me. She won't give up the baby.
> Says it's hers, and has persuaded my wife
> and daughter to admit nothing. Don't
> be surprised if I have to kill her with my bare hands.

DEMEAS
> Who? Your wife?   880

NIKERATOS
    Maybe so. She's in on the plot, too . . .

DEMEAS
    Don't do it, friend.

NIKERATOS
    I just had to warn you!
(He rushes inside again.)

DEMEAS
    He's a mad bull. Gone rushing back inside again.
    How to deal with this? Best tell him truthfully
    what's been going on? I can't remember ever being in
    such a mess. Damn me, there's the door again.

CHRYSIS
    Help. Save me! Where can I hide? He wants to
    take my baby . . .

DEMEAS
    Inside my house, angel. Run . . .   890
(She goes toward him.)

NIKERATOS
    Hey, where are you going?

DEMEAS
    Must I fight a duel with my old
    friend? Before this day's over God
    knows what may happen.
(He stands in the way of Nikeratos.)
    What do you want?
    Who are you chasing?

NIKERATOS
    Out of my way! If I can get my hands on
    that infant, the women will suddenly start to talk . . .

DEMEAS
    Never!

NIKERATOS
    You plan to fight me?   900

DEMEAS
    If necessary, yes.
    (to Chrysis)
    For God's sake, get inside my house.
    Be quick about it!

NIKERATOS
    I'll fight you for her.

DEMEAS
    Run, Chrysis. He's stronger than I am.
    (She manages to open the door to Demeas' house and get inside.)

NIKERATOS
    You started this with me. I have witnesses.

DEMEAS
    Chasing a free woman . . . trying to hit her . . .

NIKERATOS
    Slanderer.

DEMEAS
    The same to you.

NIKERATOS
    Bring out my baby.   910

DEMEAS

That's a lie. He's my grandson.

NIKERATOS

It's not . . .

DEMEAS

Oh, yes it is.

NIKERATOS

Help! Good people, all . . .

DEMEAS

Bawl your head off for all I care.

NIKERATOS

I'll take this out on my wife. I'll
murder her. That's the ticket.

DEMEAS

That's awful. I can't let you. Hey,
stop! Where are you going?

NIKERATOS

Don't you touch me.   920

DEMEAS

Control yourself!

NIKERATOS

You're playing some trick on me, Demeas.
You know something I don't know. That's clear.

DEMEAS

Ask me any questions you like. Just don't harm your wife.

NIKERATOS
> Your son's made a fool of me, hasn't he?

DEMEAS
> Rubbish! He wants the girl.
> It's not like that with him.
> *(He takes Nikeratos by the arm.)*
> Come take a turn with me . . .

NIKERATOS
> A turn?

DEMEAS
> By all means. And get a grip on yourself.   930
> Tell me, friend, have you never heard actors in a tragedy
> tell how Zeus became a stream of gold,
> poured through a roof, and seduced the
> girl who had been locked up secure?

NIKERATOS
> So what?

DEMEAS
> Does your roof leak? Be prepared for anything.

NIKERATOS
> Even if it does, what's that got to do with anything?

DEMEAS
> Sometimes Zeus is like a shower of gold, sometimes
> like rain. Do you follow me? This is his work.
> Once you know that, it's easy to accept.   940

NIKERATOS
> You're having me on.

DEMEAS

> I wouldn't dream of it. God help me. Your
> Plangon is surely just as fine as Danae. Zeus
> honored her. Why not Plangon?

NIKERATOS

> Moschion has made me a jackass!

DEMEAS

> Never fear, he'll marry Plangon. Whatever
> happened was, at least, divinely inspired.
> Thousands walking the streets of Athens
> are the children of gods. Your case is not
> exceptional. There's Chairephon, a moocher   950
> off others in restaurants and cafes. Don't
> you think the gods fathered him?

NIKERATOS

> Maybe so. I won't split hairs with you.

DEMEAS

> Now you're talking. Not to mention Androcles—
> so many years on Earth but he runs around
> like a schoolboy. A real busybody.
> He's got black hair, but even if it were
> white he'd never die, even if someone were
> to slit his throat. That's because he's
> divine. Just pray that this marriage turns   960
> out well. Burn your incense, make your
> sacrifices. Moschion will be here any minute
> to fetch his fetching bride.

NIKERATOS

> I guess I'll have to accept this.

DEMEAS

> Philosopher.

NIKERATOS

    But if I'd been around to catch him . . .

DEMEAS

    Hold your horses. Your blood pressure.
    Go in the house and get things ready for the celebration.

NIKERATOS

    As you insist.

DEMEAS

    And I will do the same in my house.   970

NIKERATOS

    Do that!

DEMEAS

    You're a smart chap.
(Nikeratos enters his house.)
    And for my jealous suspicions being
    unfounded I praise Olympus.
(He goes inside his own house. Revelers again arrive.)

CHORAL INTERLUDE

    We arrange for marrying,
    especially when there are babies.
    It isn't like when the dog bites you
    you kill it for having rabies.

    Marriage is the safest way
    to ensure neighborly harmony   980
    and keep her relatives at bay:
    We've had our fun, let's marry.

    The baby needs a legal father.
    The mother needs to be assured
    that her honor is intact
    since her maidenhead is not.

Every marriage is coerced.
Plangon's is not the worst:
Hymen's envelope was stretched
but the bride is hardly wretched.   990

Stiff upper lips, Athenian men.
Your brides will please you now and then.
Fathering will bring you joys,
and for the rest there's always boys.

ACT V

(Enter Moschion.)

MOSCHION

I'm furious! Even after my good name has been
cleared of the charge so wrongly laid against
me, I feel indignant. At first I was pleased,
thought myself lucky. But after some reflection
I've had second thoughts. That Demeas should have
thought me capable of such behavior . . .   1000
I'm absolutely livid. If it weren't for my promise,
my love for Plangon, and our relationship,
(things that leave me without choices), he and
that bully Nikeratos certainly wouldn't be making
such charges against me. Not to my face! I'd
be out of here, out of his way, in Bactria,
or someplace like that, a soldier of fortune,
living by my sword. But no such heroics now.
I've sworn an oath to marry Plangon. For your sake
I will obey, for the sake of Love, which is the master   1010
of my will. Darling, for you . . .
But is that any reason to ignore these insults?
I won't just let things pass. There must be some
way I could scare Demeas, even if I'm only acting,
to think I'm taking leave of this situation. Going
abroad . . . Then, in future, he'll be more careful
to take my word, and not treat me so unfairly.

I'll test his loyalties . . .
Here comes Parmenon. Just the man I want, and
just at the right moment . . .   1020
(Parmenon enters right, not seeing Moschion.)

PARMENON

What an ass I've been, Great Zeus! Beneath contempt. Really!
Having done nothing to be ashamed of,
I panicked and ran away from my master.
What had I done to justify his rage against me?
Let's examine all this unemotionally, point by point.
Item: The young master seduced Plangon, a respectable virgin.
Presumably Parmenon's not responsible for that.
Item: Through no fault of Parmenon's she got pregnant.
Item: When the baby was brought into Demeas'
house, that was Moschion's doing, not my own.   1030
Item: When the Master's mistress called herself
the mother, I had nothing to do with that ruse.
So why run off like a lily-livered ass, you
bumpkin? That was silly . . .
Item: Master Demeas threatened to brand me.
Now do you see? It doesn't really matter whether
such a punishment was deserved.
Branding just wasn't a very pretty prospect.

MOSCHION

Hey!

PARMENON

Good evening to you, young master!   1040

MOSCHION

Cut it out! Go inside and get me a sword!

PARMENON

Why? What for?

MOSCHION

>Bring me my military cloak!

PARMENON

>You're going to a costume party?

MOSCHION

>Bring it to me now!

PARMENON

>What for?

MOSCHION

>Just do as I tell you, and keep quiet about it.

PARMENON

>What's going on?

MOSCHION

>Should I get a whip and teach you to ask questions?

PARMENON

>No, I'll go, please . . .   1050

MOSCHION

>Then hurry up.
>*(Parmenon goes into the house.)*
>Father will be coming out now and, of course,
>he'll see me and beg me not to leave.
>For some time he'll just beg in vain. That's vital.
>Then, when I think it's right, I'll let myself be inveigled.
>All I need to do is remember my stage career.
>It so happens, I'm not very good at acting, but . . .
>Here we go again. There's the door and someone's coming out.

PARMENON *(entering from house)*
> You're quite behind the times on what is going
> on inside. You've got dated information, poor   1060
> intelligence. You're getting yourself into a
> snit quite unnecessarily. No need to despair.

MOSCHION
> Where's my cloak and sword?

PARMENON
> Don't you understand your wedding's underway?
(with enthusiasm)
> They're mixing the wine, burning incense,
> and have lit the offerings. The sacrifice is trussed and ready.

MOSCHION
> Trust is what this is all about, Parmenon. Where's
> my cloak and sword?

PARMENON
> They're waiting for you to come inside. For ages
> now they've been waiting. Why not fetch Plangon   1070
> right away? You're a lucky fellow with nothing to fear.
(With alarm he sees Moschion advancing on him.)
> Why are you behaving like this?

MOSCHION *(slapping Parmenon's face)*
> You outrageous oaf! Questioning your betters?

PARMENON
> What are you doing to me, little master?

MOSCHION
> Go! Get me my things.

PARMENON
> You've split my lip.

MOSCHION
> Still talking back?

PARMENON *(dabbing at his lip)*
> I'm going. A fine reward for all my service to you, I must say.

MOSCHION
> Get on with it!

PARMENON
> They really are celebrating, and waiting for you.   1080

MOSCHION
> The same old tale. Tell me another one.
> *(Parmenon goes inside.)*
> Now Demeas will come out.
> *(pauses)*
>> Ladies and gentlemen, suppose he loses
>> his temper rather than begs me to stay. That's
>> something I haven't figured on. So what do I
>> do then? Perhaps he won't, but perhaps he will.
>> Anything's possible in this household. If I
>> have to change my attitude again, I'll look like a real idiot.
> *(Parmenon comes from the house with cloak and sword.)*

PARMENON
> Here's your stuff. Enjoy.

MOSCHION
> Give them here.   1090
> *(casually)*
> Anybody in the house see you carrying this stuff?

PARMENON
> Not a soul.

MOSCHION
    No one at all?

PARMENON
    No.

MOSCHION
    Damn you!

PARMENON
    Get on your way! You make no sense.

DEMEAS *(coming out of the house)*
    Where did you say he was? Tell me.
(sees Moschion with cloak and sword)
    Good Heavens!
    What's going on?

PARMENON *(to Moschion)*
    Quick step march! Get out of here.   1100

DEMEAS
    Why the soldier outfit? What are you
    up to now? Are you going on a trip?
    Please enlighten me.

PARMENON
    As you can see, he's on the march, already
    on the road. And now I shall also say goodbye
    to those inside. I'll do that right now.
(He enters house.)

DEMEAS
    Moschion, I'm not surprised by your indignation.
    I love you for expressing yourself. You're
    hurt at being unfairly accused. But consider
    who you've made the target for such anger.   1110
    I am your father. I took you in when you

were little and brought you up as my own son.
If your life has been at all privileged and pleasant,
I'm the man who helped to make that possible.
I gave you all the advantages, and
I believe it's your duty to put up with
my unfortunate behavior, and bear with me
as a good son should,
even though I may have hurt you.

What I thought about you proved unjustified.   1120
I made a mistake. I was just plain wrong.
Out of my mind with jealousy. I admit that.
But consider this: At the cost of possibly
hurting others I still looked carefully after
the interests of my son. Tried to keep my
suspicions to myself. Did not slander you
to please our enemies. If you are trying to
embarrass me now by making my mistake public,
that's wrong, Moschion. Don't try to shame me.
That's not fair. It was just one bad day in   1130
our lives when I was out of my mind with jealousy.
But think of our whole life together before
that as father and son.

I could say a lot more to you, but I'll let
it go at that, Moschion. Now, you let it go,
lad. Sons get no credit for reluctant obedience.
Forgive and forget gladly. That's the only way.
(*Enter Nikeratos from his house, talking over his shoulder.*)

NIKERATOS
    Stop nagging me. All is ready: baths,
    ritual music, wedding ceremonies, the lot.
    If he ever shows his face, the bridegroom   1140
    can take the bride away.
(*notices the others*)
    My heavens! What's happening here now?

DEMEAS
>I assure you, I don't know.

NIKERATOS
>Something's up. Mufti.
>He must be going off somewhere.

DEMEAS
>That's what I assume.

NIKERATOS
>He's got to be stopped. He can't evade it.
>He's a seducer, caught in the act after
>taking advantage. His guilt is plain.
>I'll arrest him on the spot.   1150

MOSCHION *(drawing his sword)*
>Just try to arrest me!

NIKERATOS
>I am serious. Put up your sword at once.

DEMEAS
>For God's sake, Moschion, don't taunt him.
>Put up your sword.

MOSCHION *(sheathing his sword again)*
>Oh, there! Let it go. I've complied with
>your appeals to me.

NIKERATOS
>Appeals? Come here, you!

MOSCHION
>You still think you'll arrest me?

DEMEAS
  Stop this shamming. Bring out the bride!

NIKERATOS
  Are you sure?   1160

DEMEAS
  Quite!
(Nikeratos enters the house.)

MOSCHION
  Father, if you'd trusted me more you wouldn't have
  had to bother with your recent sermon.

NIKERATOS *(returning with Plangon in hand)*
  After you dear.
(Members of both households assemble.)
  In the presence of witnesses,
  Moschion, I give you this woman to be
  your wife for the procreation of legitimate
  children. And as dowry I give her all
  my possessions when I die (God forbid!
  May I live forever!)   1170

MOSCHION
  I take her to have, to hold, and to cherish.

DEMEAS
  It remains that we fetch the ritual water,
  Chrysis. Call out the women, the water carrier,
  and the musician. Someone bring us a torch
  and proper garlands so we may make a procession.

MOSCHION *(as these things arrive)*
  Here they come.

DEMEAS
Put on your garland, son, and deck yourself like a bridegroom.

MOSCHION
There!
(Chorus of revelers reappears.)

CHORUS
Every swain is a goat!
Every goat is a swain.   1180
The World made right,
let's bring on Night,
and lovers to their arms again.

DEMEAS *(to the audience, including the revelers)*
Pretty lads, young men, old guys, ladies
and gentlemen, all together now—please
clap loudly. Dionysus loves applause.
It shows you love our play. May Victory,
immortal patron of our finest festivals,
grant perpetual favor to this company.
(They exit in procession and the Chorus recapitulates its final interlude.)

The Shield (Aspis)

Translated by
Sheila D'Atri and Palmer Bovie

Translators' Preface

The *Aspis*, here *The Shield*, is a tragicomedy of the late fourth century B.C. It was written sometime soon after the death of Alexander the Great when his generals frequently fought for control of the southern coast of Asia Minor. Much money was spent on the expeditions, freebooting was the rule, and young men signed up in droves to fight as mercenaries. We know that a great number of them lost their lives. Although it is impossible to know whether any particular historical battle forms the reference point for the play, the general situation in Lycia is clear.

The play opens in Athens. Daos, the faithful slave and tutor of Kleostratos, appears carrying a battered shield that had belonged to his master. With him are captives from Lycia and a great deal of property in the form of gold, vessels, and fabrics that were taken by Kleostratos in battle. Daos has returned from the battleground grieving the death of his master. He has identified the body (a few days dead) that was holding the shield as that of Kleostratos. He also tells us in the first scene that the reason his master went to war was to win a sufficient dowry for his sister.

Trouble shows up soon after Daos' arrival in the person of Smikrines, Kleostratos' uncle. He is a classic avaricious old man. Drooling at the loot, he claims it his right to marry the sister of Kleostratos (not named in the play). As her oldest surviving relative, he becomes her official "protector." In that capacity, he intends to win the dowry by marrying her himself. Meanwhile the girl and a young man named Chaireas love each other. Chaireas is the stepson of Chairestratos, the younger brother of Smikrines.

How will the young couple and their friends prevail? How will they foil the wicked Smikrines? We know that they will win. After all, this is a comedy, and nothing is left to chance. Actually, everything is left to Chance, for the goddess Chance herself (the Greek Tyche) appears in person after the first scene to explain the true situation to the audience. We learn, long before the characters do, that Kleostratos is not dead. In the quick onset of battle the soldiers grabbed whatever weapons were handy, and that is how Daos came by later (after depositing the booty in a safe place at his master's bidding) to find an unrecognizable corpse with his master's shield.

Kleostratos, who has been held captive, returns well before the end of the drama. Before this, Daos the slave will come to the rescue in a plot within the plot, a play within the play. He and Chairestratos lure Smikrines away with promises of even greater riches in the person of Chairestratos' daughter. Chairestratos has actually been ill with severe depression over the loss of his nephew and sorrow over his niece's misfortune. Daos persuades him to turn fact into fiction and carry it still further—Chairestratos is to feign a sickness unto death, and they get a fake doctor to add comic exaggeration to the proceedings. Smikrines, lured by greed and the hope of Chairestratos' greater fortunes falling into his hands, renounces his first choice—he is glad now to hand her over to Chaireas.

By the time Kleostratos returns home, the fun is done and also made unnecessary. Poignant confusions rule for a while. Daos, thinking that Kleostratos is a stranger at the gate, tells him to go away, that Chairestratos has died. It is now Kleostratos, to mourn without cause. But soon, in shock, Daos recognizes him, and Kleostratos is home to give his sister to her beloved and to marry the daughter of Chairestratos himself. The play ends with a double wedding and celebration for all except Smikrines, who skulks off feeling victimized. Character, logic, and Chance unite to produce a happy ending.

Cast

DAOS, an old slave, former tutor to Kleostratos
SMIKRINES, uncle of Kleostratos
TYCHE, goddess of Chance
COOK
TABLE-SETTER
CHORUS of revelers
CHAIRESTRATOS, younger brother of Smikrines
CHAIREAS, stepson of Chairestratos
SOSTRATOS, friend disguised as a doctor
KLEOSTRATOS, son of a dead brother of Smikrines and
    Chairestratos
NEIGHBOR
NONSPEAKING
    Captives
    Sparks, cook's assistant
    "Doctor"'s assistant
    Neighbors
    Slaves

*(The scene is a street in Athens. Two houses belonging to the
brothers Smikrines and Chairestratos are next to one another on
the stage.)*

ACT I

*(Daos enters carrying a battered shield. With him are captives and
animals carrying war booty. Smikrines is in the alleyway
watching and listening, unseen by Daos.)*

DAOS *(speaking to the absent Kleostratos)*
    O my dear, my foster-child,
    I pass this day bereaved
    of all the hopes I had when we sailed off.
    I thought you'd come back safe and well-respected—

this expedition ended and you'd spend
the remainder of your life in luxury.
You'd be called a general or counselor,
and your sister, for whose sake you once set sail,
would be married to a much-desired bridegroom
upon your coming home.   10
And, as for me, I hoped for rest as I grow old
from all my lengthy laboring,
counting on your kindness.
But now you're dead, senselessly slaughtered,
and I, your tutor, O Kleostratos, have come,
not saving you, but holding here this shield,
which oftentimes was saved by you.
You were a man of unmatched spirit,
No one could compare with you.

SMIKRINES *(coming out of the alley toward Daos at center stage)*
   O Daos, what an unexpected misfortune!   20

DAOS
   Dreadful.

SMIKRINES
   In what way did he die?

DAOS
   In the army, Smikrines, they say safety is difficult
   and destruction is an easy path to find.

SMIKRINES
   But Daos, tell me how it came about.

DAOS
   There's a river named Xanthus in the land of Lycia.
   We fought there many times successfully.
   The natives had run and left the plain to us.

Sometimes it seems it's better
not to be lucky all the time.   30
The man who falls remains on guard.
Without thinking, without order, we rushed
toward the future. Many had left the camp
to raid the towns; they felled the crops,
they sold the spoils, and each returned
with masses of money and loot.

SMIKRINES

Sounds good to me!

DAOS

And he himself, the master who took care of me,
was bringing back six hundred coins of gold
and many drinking-cups, and this huge crowd of captives   40
which you see right here.
He sent me to Rhodes and told me to leave them
with his friend there and then to turn around
and hurry back to him.

SMIKRINES

And then what happened?

DAOS

I started at dawn, but on that day
those on the watch had failed to notice
the natives who had grabbed the hill above us
and remained. They learned about our scattered strength
from some of our deserters. Then at evening—   50
the whole army back in the tents, having it all,
what happened was the usual—
most of them were drinking heavily.

SMIKRINES

That's really bad!

DAOS

> I think it hit them suddenly.
> There seemed to be a rout.

SMIKRINES

> So what did you find there?

DAOS

> It was the middle of the night
> when I arrived, standing guard
> over our possessions and our slaves,   60
> when in front of the tent I heard
> noises, cries of pain, and shouting,
> as men called each other's names.
> And then I heard what happened.
> With some good luck there was a little hill,
> and all of us could crowd on top
> while our wounded army filtered in,
> bearing our guards and horsemen.

SMIKRINES

> Lucky for you that you'd been sent away.

DAOS

> At dawn we constructed a fortification,   70
> and there we stayed. Those who'd been scattered
> now kept coming back to us. On the fourth day
> we set off again. The Lycians—so we heard—
> were taking our captured men
> to towns they held up high in the mountains.

SMIKRINES

> And did you see your master
> fallen among the bodies?

DAOS

> I couldn't recognize him clearly.
> It was the fourth day since they'd fallen—
> the faces were swollen.   80

SMIKRINES

> So how did you know?

DAOS

> Holding his shield, he lay there on the ground.
> The shield was battered in, and I suppose
> The natives had no use for it.
> Our noble leader forbade us
> from burning our own, one at a time.
> There was no time to waste
> in gathering the bones of each, and so,
> all massed together for cremation,
> we buried them in haste.   90
> First we went to Rhodes and stayed there
> for some days, and then we sailed back here.
> And now you have heard it all.

SMIKRINES

> Six hundred pieces of gold
> you say you brought?

DAOS

> I have.

SMIKRINES

> And drinking cups?

DAOS

> Weighted at forty . . . now wait,
> for you—I see just now—have your designs
> upon his newly wealthy sister.   100

SMIKRINES *(pauses, then looks at the pack animals)*
>How's that? Do you think I asked
>for a reason like that? By Apollo!
>And the rest was snatched away?

DAOS
>Most of it, except for what I took at first.
>There are cloaks in there and chlamydes,
>and this whole crowd you see
>now is added to your household goods.

SMIKRINES *(smugly)*
>I don't care about all those things.
>A man like that should have lived.

DAOS
>He should have.   110
>Now let's go inside
>to tell this wretched story
>to those who for whom it matters most.

SMIKRINES
>And then, at your leisure, Daos,
>I'd like to talk to you.
>*(Daos goes into Chairestratos' house. Alone on the stage, Smikrines*
>   *speaks to the audience and then enters his own*
>   *house.)*
>And now I'll take myself inside
>to work out the ways that I might make
>the most urbane approach.
>*(The goddess of Chance, Tyche, now appears and addresses the*
>   *audience.)*

TYCHE
>If something awful had really happened
>to those good people you've seen,   120

it never would be seemly
for a goddess like me to follow them here.
Now they know nothing and wander about,
but you come close and learn from me
what really did take place.
There was another, a friend of the master,
who shared his things and stayed close by
at the time when the natives attacked—
and the shouts sounded out and the signals to arm—
and each took what armor was closest to hand.   130
So that's how it happened that he who tried to help
our friend was carrying his shield.
Right away he fell, and later, when that young man lay
swollen among the bodies,
holding the shield at his side,
Daos arrived, utterly appalled and mistaken.
As for our Kleostratos—
he'd joined the ranks with borrowed arms
and then became a captive.
But still he lives and will be saved,   140
although not yet. You've learned enough about him.
As for that old man who's searching through the lot—
he's our hero's uncle and a most accomplished work
of villainy. He has no respect
for friend or relation, but considers nothing
to be shameful in his life. He wants to have it all.
That's all he knows.
He lives by himself, with one old woman in attendance.
The neighboring house, where Daos has just gone,
belongs to the younger brother of that money-grubber.   150
He also is the young man's uncle,
but he is good as well as wealthy,
and has a wife and an unmarried daughter.
Kleostratos put his sister in his care
when he went off to war.
The two young girls were raised together here,

and, as I said, he is a wealthy man.
Now when he saw how long his nephew would be gone
and the limits of his household goods,
he intended for his niece be married   160
to the son of his wife by her former husband.
He'd planned to give two talents as a dowry,
and the marriage was supposed to be NOW.
This news will drop like a rock into that plan.
That rotten egg you saw has heard of gold
and looked at foreign slaves and mules and girls,
and, since the sister's now an heiress,
he wants to rule the roost
and triumph through seniority.
His efforts will all be for nothing,   170
his actions will reveal his nature,
and he'll go back to what he was before.
All that remains is to tell you my name.
I make the judgments and the dispensations—
I am Tyche, also known as Lady Luck.
(Tyche leaves the stage just as Smikrines is seen coming out of his house.)

SMIKRINES
So no one can call me a money-lover.
I didn't go through the load of gold or silver cups.
I made no count of anything, letting them bring it in there.
They're accustomed to disparage me for everything.
The amount cannot be found, in any case,   180
since those who brought it in are slaves.
I must believe that my people will follow the law
and abide by what's right.
If not, then nothing will go forward.
The impending wedding I will stop.
Perhaps it's needless to say,
but when word of wealth appears
there are no weddings for paupers.
(pauses, then goes to the door of his neighbor's house)

Now I'll knock and summon Daos out.
He'll certainly pay heed to me.   190

DAOS *(coming out, speaking to someone inside)*
    I understand your reactions—given what's happened—
    but try to bear up like a man.

SMIKRINES
    Daos, I've come here for you.

DAOS
    For me?

SMIKRINES
    Yes, by Zeus. Your master should have lived,
    since he was just, and according to the law
    he would have been executor
    of all my goods when I am gone.

DAOS
    He ought to have. So what?

SMIKRINES
    Well then—I am the oldest of our clan, yet unjustly   200
    I see my brother take over for me.

DAOS *(in disbelief)*
    Are you out of your mind?

SMIKRINES
    My friend—he's so immoderate—
    Does he think me a home-wrecker or some kind of bastard,
    that he'd marry her off to I don't know whom?
    He didn't consider my opinion at all,
    but I'm the same kin, her uncle as well.

DAOS

    What's that about?

SMIKRINES

    I'm furious, seeing all this.
    Since he acts like a stranger to me, I'll do the same to him.   210
    I won't leave my wealth for them to weasel away.
    I had some advice to marry the girl myself,
    and I think the law bears me out, Daos, in this.
    As the eldest relation, I have rights.
    Even you should see it's the right thing to do,
    and the right way to think. You're no stranger here.

DAOS

    Smikrines—the old expression "know thyself"
    seems to be important here. Let me rest with that.
    Ask me about the things that matter
    to a slave who can be trusted. You own our bodies;   220
    don't request advice on matters that concern you citizens.
    I can tell you what commercial ventures
    Kleostratos set up before he left.
    These things (if someone asks me) I will show,
    and where and how, with whom,
    but as for weddings and inheritance
    and household disagreements,
    don't put Daos in the middle.
    Men should act on what pertains to them.

SMIKRINES

    By the gods, do you think I'm missing the mark?   230

DAOS

    I'm Phrygian. Much of what seems good to you
    is the opposite to me. Why do you care what I say?
    Of course your thoughts are much better than mine.

SMIKRINES

    I think you're saying "don't involve me,"
    or something like that. I understand.
    I'm off to the market to see if my brother is there,
    since he doesn't seem to be inside.
(Smikrines sets off for the agora. Daos is alone on stage, muttering a
prayer to the goddess of Chance.)

DAOS

    No worse master, Lady Luck, could you have sent
    after one like Kleostratos.
    Oh, what did I do to deserve this?   240
(Cook comes out of Chairestratos' house with his assistant Sparks.)

COOK

    Whatever work I undertake,
    either the undertaker gets the fee instead
    and I go off without my pay,
    or some woman who's secretly pregnant
    gives birth and off I go again. Misery's my fate.

DAOS

    By the gods! Cook—go away.

COOK

    What do you think I am doing?
(to Sparks)
    Take the knives, boy, and quickly for once.
    I signed on for this work a dozen days ago—
    three drachmas was the fee—I thought I had them in my hand.   250
    And now a corpse from Lycia has snatched them off by force.
    When catastrophe like that has hit,
    remember opportunity and take it.
    Do you see the weeping women beating their breasts
    and leave without taking a thing? Sparks, you robber of graves,
    is it you or Aristides the Just

that I have for a helper?
I'll see that you have no supper tonight.
(Table-setter comes out from the house.)
Perhaps this servant will stay,
taking his chance on a funeral feast.   260
(Table-setter speaks to the cook as he is leaving.)

TABLE-SETTER
If I don't grab my drachmas now,
I'll tear myself apart no less than you.

DAOS *(to table-setter)*
Oh, go away! You're another nuisance here.

TABLE-SETTER
Shouldn't it be that I come first to me?

DAOS
Most certainly.

TABLE-SETTER
Then take your ugly self away, by Zeus!
What have you done? Were you struck *dumb*
by so much gold and slaves
that you come back *here* with it all
and offer it back to your masters!   270
You didn't run off? From where do you come?

DAOS
From Phrygia.

TABLE-SETTER
There's nothing respectable there—a place for womanly men.
Only we Thracians are male. Yes, by Apollo,
We Getai alone possess the right stuff.
That's why we fill up the mills
and suffer the weight of the heaviest loads.

DAOS
> Just get your Getic feet from the door—and scram.

(Table-setter leaves.)
> I see another crowd of men, and they look tipsy.
> What they do makes sense. The future's dim,   280
> so why not be as happy as you can
> in the time you have?

(Chorus of revelers comes on for the interlude between the acts, singing
the refrain of a drinking song.)

CHORUS
> We'll worship Bacchus and the vine,
> with little water in our wine;
> let's keep away the thoughts of death,
> imbibe without a stop for breath.

ACT II

> *(Smikrines, his brother Chairestratos, and Chaireas, Chairestratos'*
> *stepson, enter after the Chorus leaves.)*

SMIKRINES
> So what do you say now, Chairestratos?

CHAIRESTRATOS *(sarcastically)*
> O best of men, at first
> we need to be busy with the burial.

SMIKRINES
> We will get busy with it.   290
> But, after that, agree to give the girl to no one.
> This is a matter for me and not for you.
> I'm the elder, while you have a wife
> and also a daughter indoors.
> It ought to be the same for me.

CHAIRESTRATOS
> Smikrines, does moderation mean a thing to you?

SMIKRINES
    Why, my boy?

CHAIRESTRATOS
    Given the age that you've reached,
    do you really intend to marry a girl?

SMIKRINES
    How old do you think I seem?   300

CHAIRESTRATOS
    To me you seem completely a geezer.

SMIKRINES
    Am I alone among older men to want to take a wife?

CHAIRESTRATOS
    Bear with this business in a manly manner,
    by the gods, O Smikrines!
(points to Chaireas standing by his side)
    Chaireas here has grown up with the girl,
    always intending to make her his wife.
    What can I tell you? You won't lose a thing.
    Take all the booty, whatever there is—
    you be in charge of it all, we give it to you.
    But as for the girl, she's young, let her find   310
    a partner for marriage that's like her in age.
    From my own belongings I'll provide
    a dowry of two talents.

SMIKRINES
    By the gods, do you suppose that you are babbling
    to a fool? What are you saying?
    That I should take the stuff, give up the girl,
    and then—if and when they have a son—
    I'll be sued for having what belongs to him?

CHAIRESTRATOS
Is that what you think? Just let that thought go.

SMIKRINES
"Think," you say? Send Daos to me   320
to prepare a list of the booty.

CHAIRESTRATOS
What more can possibly be done?

SMIKRINES
I want to be sure that what's mine is mine.
(Smikrines goes into his house.)

CHAIRESTRATOS *(to Chaireas)*
I always believed you'd marry this girl
and Kleostratos would marry my daughter—
and I would leave my property to both of you.
I wish I could quit this life right now
before I see my hopes disintegrate.
(Chairestratos in despair goes into his house. Chaireas, who has been
silent until now, speaks.)

CHAIREAS
So it is. Oh, first, Kleostratos,
we must mourn what you have suffered   330
and weep and speak your due.
But the second misery is mine,
for no one's had misfortune quite like mine.
Falling in love with your sister was not a matter of choice,
dear friend, who was dearest to me.
I did nothing rash or illicit, but asked your uncle
if I could wed with proper ceremony.
You'd left her in his care, and with my mother as well,
who brought her up from childhood.
I thought my life was fortunate—   340

I'd just about accomplished my wish—
and now I'm not even able to see her.
The law awards her to another husband
and I am left with nothing.
(Daos appears at Chairestratos' door and speaks to Chairestratos inside.)

DAOS

Chairestratos, you're not behaving well. Stand up!
You can't just lie there like a log that has no life.
(approaches Chaireas and speaks to him)
Chaireas, come and say a word to him.
Don't let him fail—for this whole matter
that involves us all may yet find help from him.
(calls inside again to Chairestratos)
Open the door—put yourself in evidence.   350
Chairestratos, will you behave
as though you had no family
and do this to the people who love you?
(Chairestratos staggers out of the house.)

CHAIRESTRATOS

Daos, my boy, I'm sick.
This business has made me more that melancholy.
By the gods, I'm not myself. I'm so depressed,
I'm mad. That fine evil brother of mine
has made me go out of my mind—
For *he* intends to get married.

DAOS

Tell me, will he be able to marry?   360

CHAIRESTRATOS

So that paragon of virtue seems to say—
even though I offered all my nephew sent.

DAOS

Oh, he's out and out pollution!

CHAIRESTRATOS
> Yes, a polluted poison. By the gods,
> I won't be alive to see this happen.

DAOS
> So how can we circumvent this villain?

CHAIRESTRATOS
> With a ton of bricks?

DAOS
> Still not impossible.

CHAIRESTRATOS
> You think it's possible?

DAOS
> The effort, by Athena, would make a worthy victory.   370

CHAIRESTRATOS
> If only someone . . . by the gods . . .
> could undertake some plot or plan.

DAOS
> A plan is what we need—let's think.
> He hopes to get two talents with this bride—
> Let's show him more, and let him fall
> right on his sinful face. He'll take one look
> and take his defeat in his hands.
> A man who thinks only of himself
> loses his reason and the sense to judge the truth.

CHAIRESTRATOS *(looking alive again)*
> What are you saying? For now I am ready   370
> to do whatever it is that you wish.

DAOS

> You must act your part as though it were
> within a tragedy. What you have said before
> must now appear to be. You must fall
> into a lifeless state, due to all the agony you feel
> over Kleostratos and Chaireas and the girl he thought was his.
> When you saw Chaireas depressed to death—
> a boy you'd considered your son—
> well all of a sudden you're shaken,
> and then you fall into shock.   390
> The greatest sickness, after all, is said to come from grief.
> And I know well that this black bile
> lies truly within your nature.
> You will play an exaggerated self.
> Then we get a doctor in—a philosophizing kind of foreigner—
> who'll call it pleurisy or phrenic-type malignancy
> or something else that's bound to kill the victim.

CHAIRESTRATOS

> What then?

DAOS

> You've suddenly died. We shout
> "Chairestratos has gone," and strike ourselves   400
> in front of the doors of your house.
> We shut you away while a wrapped up
> mummy will lie in state instead of you.

CHAIRESTRATOS *(to Chaireas in amazement)*

> Do you understand what he's talking about?

CHAIREAS

> By Dionysus, I don't!

CHAIRESTRATOS

> Neither do I.

DAOS

> Now your daughter, too, according to the law,
> bears a substantial legacy,
> like the girl we talked about before.
> But you're worth sixty talents   410
> and Kleostratos' estate comes just to four.
> The greedy geezer's uncle to them both.

CHAIRESTRATOS *(suddenly perking up)*

> *Now* I understand!

DAOS

> If you don't have a rock for a head,
> he'll gladly give the first girl away
> to the first one who asks,
> even before three thousand witnesses,
> thinking to capture the other.

CHAIRESTRATOS *(interrupting)*

> He should only choke!

DAOS

> Or so he thinks. He'll make his rounds   420
> around the house, getting the keys, sealing the doors,
> all in his dream of riches.

CHAIRESTRATOS

> And what about the phantom me?

DAOS

> It will lie. All of us will sit in a circle
> and stop him from getting too close.
> There are other advantages here—
> you'll be able to draw out your friends
> and find out why each of them comes to the house.
> What if one is a debtor? If he makes off with anything,
> you'll exact a double penalty from him.   430

CHAIRESTRATOS
    You've spoken splendidly, Daos,
    with wiles that appeal to my nature.
    So what excess of revenge do you plan
    for that wretched monster of a man?

DAOS
    I'll exact, by Zeus, a worthy reward
    for all the pain he's ever given you.
    The saying is true of the wolf—
    that his muzzle is gaping but goes away empty.
    And now it's time to act.
    Chaireas, do you know any foreign doctor—   440
    one who is savvy to play an imposter?

CHAIREAS
    By Zeus, not at all.

DAOS
    Well, you ought to know *someone*—

CHAIREAS
    What about this—I'll go and get one of my friends,
    and ask for a cloak and a wig and a staff,
    and tell him to mutter outlandishly,
    as much as he is able.

DAOS
    Hurry up, then.

CHAIRESTRATOS
    What about me—what should I do?

DAOS
    Those are the plans. Die, and good luck.   450

CHAIRESTRATOS

> I'll do it! Let no one go outside,
> but guard this matter manfully!

DAOS

> But who should share this secret with us?

CHAIRESTRATOS

> Only my wife and the girls must be told,
> or else they will mourn me in fact.
> But as for the others, let all the servants
> think me a corpse, and I will see how they behave.

DAOS

> You've got it right.
> *(calls into the house for some help)*
> Let someone come and help the master get inside.
> *(The slaves come out and help a feeble looking Chairestratos back into*
> *the house.)*
> This incident may give us all manner of amusement   460
> and a game that will go out of bounds.
> That is, if it ever gets going,
> and our "doctor" is able to be persuasive.
> *(Daos goes into Chairestratos' house and the Chorus of revelers takes over*
> *the stage.)*

CHORUS

> Eros with his golden curls
> threw out to me a golden ball
> and persuaded me to call
> upon a purple-sandaled girl.
> I must be drunk, my hair is white,
> she yawns at me, won't spend the night.

ACT III

(Smikrines comes out of his house as the Chorus leaves, looking annoyed.)

SMIKRINES

Daos has surely come quickly with that list   470
of the loot that I asked him to bring.
So this is what he thinks of me!
I think he's gone over to *them*.
Well, by Zeus, the stuff looks good.
Actually, I'm glad to count it out myself.
I need a pretext for my benefit—
not to put too fine a face on it—
but surely somewhere there is twice this property
that he's put where I can't see.
I know the tricks of a slave!   480

DAOS *(coming out of Chairestratos' house and ignoring Smikrines)*
O Gods. It's fearful, by the Sun, what happened.
I never would have thought
a man could fall as fast as that. A raging thunderbolt
has fallen straight upon the house.

SMIKRINES *(to himself)*
What does he want? Whatever does he mean?
Is this man mad?

DAOS *(quoting tragedy)*
"No man is always happy in all things."
(That's a great poetic line.) O honored gods,
this business was so unforeseeable!

SMIKRINES *(approaching him)*
Daos, you lout—where are you off to?   490

DAOS *(ignoring him)*
>And also this—"Fate settles the affairs of men, not prudence."
>(Another great line.) "A god plants the cause in mortals
>when he wishes evil to destroy a house completely."
>It was Aeschylus who said those godlike words.

SMIKRINES
>Reciting speeches, you wretch?

DAOS *(ignoring him)*
>"Without faith, without sense, awful, terrible . . ."

SMIKRINES
>Will he never stop?

DAOS
>"What of human miseries remains beyond belief?"
>That's what Carcinus says. "For in one day
>the god can make the fortunate unfortunate."   500
>*(turning to Smikrines)*
>These are well-spoken, Smikrines.

SMIKRINES
>What are you talking about?

DAOS
>Your brother, O Zeus, how can I phrase it?
>He's close to death.

SMIKRINES
>The one who was just chatting with me?
>What happened to him?

DAOS
>Bile, some sort of pain, going out of his mind,
>and choking.

SMIKRINES
    Poseidon and the gods, how horrible!

DAOS
    "There is nothing neither horrible to tell,   510
    no suffering . . ."

SMIKRINES
    You're wearing me out.

DAOS
    "The gods have decreed that tragedies
    come unpredictably." The former is Euripides,
    the latter's Chaeremon. Not just anybody.

SMIKRINES
    Did a doctor happen to come?

DAOS
    None. But Chaireas has gone to get one.

SMIKRINES
    Who is that?
(Chaireas and Sostratos the "doctor," followed by his assistant, head
across the stage to Chairestratos' house.)

DAOS *(pointing)*
    There they are, by Zeus, as it appears.
(to Sostratos)
    O best of men, hurry in, please.   520

SOSTRATOS
    I'm goink as fest as I kin.

DAOS
    "The sick are hard to please because of their misfortunes."
(Daos follows the others into Chairestratos' house. Smikrines waits
anxiously on stage.)

SMIKRINES

    If they see me right away, right away they'll say
    I came because I'm pleased. This I understand.
    Even my brother himself might turn sour
    seeing me here at his sickbed.

(paces)

    But still it would be strange to stay away.
    I should at least be asking after him
    in circumstances such as these.
    Fraternal feelings do not fail—   530
    and so I will approach his house.

(Smikrines starts to knock at Chairestratos' door when the "doctor"
comes out, speaking to his assistant.)

SOSTRATOS

    Und zo ve zee hiss bile iss bad
    und zo he may not liff zo long
    vit hiss condition az ve zee it iss.

SMIKRINES *(chasing alongside and addressing the "doctor")*

    What's that you say? I hardly understood.

SOSTRATOS

    I zaid it's *zerious.*

SMIKRINES

    That at least I understand.

SOSTRATOS

    It zeems to me hiss inzides are a mess.
    Hiss diaphragm zuffers hepaticomegaly.
    Hiss brain iss inflamed, zo ve are accustomed   540
    to call ziss condition . . .

SMIKRINES

    I understand. What next? Is there any hope of cure?

SOSTRATOS
>There iss a time that comes . . .
>I muss not encourage your hopes
>vit empty vords.

SMIKRINES
>Don't encourage. Only tell the truth.

SOSTRATOS
>He hass not much of life left to liff.
>Ze bile iss rizink up on him
>und darkness closes on hiss eyes.
>He's bristled vit chills comink constantly   550
>und he looks like he's lookink at hiss burial.

SMIKRINES
>How horrible!

SOSTRATOS *(to assistant)*
>Ve should go now, boy.

SMIKRINES
>Wait . . . hey . . . you . . . you . . .

SOSTRATOS
>You call me back again?

SMIKRINES
>Yes I do. Come here a moment
>and step away from the door.

SOSTRATOS
>Meanvile, you shouldn't liff as you do.

SMIKRINES
>Oh, get away, now you should pray
>to be as fit as me. And yet alas   560
>it's true that all things come to pass.

SOSTRATOS
    Go laugh. I say I haff ze art of liffink well.
    But you I think to have a dissease—
    a vastink avay dissease. You're in decay.
    Und alzo you look like altogether death.
    (Sostratos stomps off with the assistant. Smikrines is alone on stage.)

SMIKRINES
    That house will be like property
    taken in wartime. The women there will carry
    all they can move to the neighbors
    and organize their thieving channels
    even along the sewers.   570
    (Daos comes out of Chairestratos' house and at first speaks to the
    audience.)

DAOS
    I'll make him weep, just wait and see—
    what I have done is nothing yet.
    (approaches Smikrines and speaks to him, feigning grief)
    O Smikrines, a tragedy is happening—
    we must bear up and try to live without him,
    and as the leader of the family, we all look to you.

SMIKRINES
    I must see him and then see to things
    that he would want me now to do.

DAOS
    He's resting now, but very ill, his brain's inflamed,
    and yet he utters his concerns for all his family.
    You have his blessing now, he said,   580
    to wed the sister of Kleostratos,
    but as the elder of the family
    he puts his trust in you to find
    a suitable match for his daughter.

SMIKRINES

His daughter! Oh, yes . . . the girl is to be fatherless.
Daos, I must see she's cared for.

DAOS

Chairestratos has provided well for her
and also for his wife. His estate is worth
some sixty talents, maybe more,
and still they lack a protector.   590

SMIKRINES

Why, I'll protect them all—I'll decide it all,
all for the sake of poor Chairestratos,
and for the preservation of what's theirs.
(Smikrines paces nervously about the stage, talking to himself. Daos
stands to one side, watching and concealing a
smile.)
Sixty talents! And I would have settled for four.
His daughter needs a father; I'd be like a father to her.
The other girl will be much better off
if she's with someone else.
Now—how to resolve this with Daos—
he's just a slave, but people seem to listen to him here.
(Smikrines goes over to Daos, looking earnest.)
Daos, my duty is clear. I will announce to Chaireas   600
that he may have the sister of Kleostratos.
I will remand her to his care. I will do all
Chairestratos had wished and more indeed.

DAOS

You needn't give up the girl that you love.
You made your devotion very clear,
and now that you're in charge of all of us
it's only right that you do right by you.

SMIKRINES *(to himself)*

How do I unravel this and look sincere?
They'll think that I'm after the money
while I'm playing the part of pater familias.   610
(to Daos)

Daos, my duty is clear, as I said,
and I must do as I see fit to do.
Now you must call Chaireas and witnesses,
so he can proceed with his plans,
although no one can think of weddings just now.
Family grief comes first and festivities later.
I need to console where I can, and I will come
with you to my brother and offer assurance.

DAOS

He's not up to hearing much. If you go in,
keep your speech to a minimum, for his bile   620
has congested his spleen. Keep a distance,
and don't upset him with plans and decisions.
(Smikrines goes into Chairestratos' house. Daos remains on stage.)

DAOS

My fish is hooked. His greed is choking him.
He's hardly aware of how awful he looks
as he looks toward the wealthier girl
and tries to seem magnanimous.
Soon I'll have him swear in front of witnesses
that Chaireas will wed the girl he loves.
*(Chorus of revelers starts to cross the stage as Daos goes into
Chairestratos' house.)*

CHORUS

Eros the lord god of love has subdued me
with the aid of the Nymphs and Aphrodite.   630
I have begged the gorgeous Kleoboulos
to love me, so help me Dionysus.

ACT IV

(Chaireas, Daos, Smikrines, and two neighbors come out of
Chairestratos' house.)

SMIKRINES *(smirking grandly)*
    You have heard me. In the midst of tragedy
    we know that life goes on. We wait in pain,
    as the lifeblood of Chairestratos
    seeps away from his soul and we all grieve
    for him and his wife and his daughter.
    The waiting is hard for all of us,
    and yet we must hold fast, be strong, and wait
    to accept whatever fate or chance may bring.   640
    Perhaps a miracle will come—
    the doctor may be mistaken, and yet
    we must prepare as best we can. And so
    you've all heard me say as head of the family
    that Chaireas shall someday soon, as planned,
    take for wife the sister of Kleostratos,
    my nephew who has died in war . . .
(Suddenly a great shout is heard from inside Chairestratos' house.)

DAOS
    They're shouting and crying inside.
(runs to the door of the house)
    They are wailing "Chairestratos has died."
    He's gone, the man is no more, we're left behind.   650
    We must be ready to endure the unendurable.

SMIKRINES *(taking charge)*
    Now we must enter the house.
    My brother found no miracle,
    and we must prepare a burial.
(They all go into the house. Soon afterward Smikrines leaves, looking
                      distracted.)

SMIKRINES

    They hardly let me near him. I'm afraid
    I must be careful. I want my marriage
    to proceed without undue objection.
    Now I must prepare my papers and my thoughts.
(Smikrines goes into his own house. The stage is empty for a short while.
        Then Kleostratos, the nephew presumed dead,
        appears, coming from the harbor.)

KLEOSTRATOS

    O dearest land, I'm home again!
    I've prayed so many times for this   660
    and now I'm here, I'm home. And yet I need
    to hope my luck has held a little more
    and Daos has returned in safety here.
    I'd think myself most fortunate of men
    if only this were true. So now I'll knock
    and see who's here. Servants, come, the door is locked.
(He knocks at Chairestratos' door and hears Daos' voice through the
        locked door.)

DAOS

    Who are you?

KLEOSTRATOS

    It's me.

DAOS

    Who do you want? Go away.
    The master of the house has died.   670

KLEOSTRATOS

    He's died? Oh, great misfortune, Oh, alas.

DAOS

    You go away, and don't give grief
    to those of us who mourn.

KLEOSTRATOS
  Oh, I am lost in woe, O uncle dear—
  and you, you wretched fool, now open up the door.

DAOS *(opening the door)*
  Go off, my boy . . .
(nearly falls back, not believing his eyes)
  O Zeus, can I believe my eyes?

KLEOSTRATOS
  Daos, what are you saying?

DAOS *(stunned, in shock, then grabbing Kleostratos in his arms)*
  I'm really holding you!

KLEOSTRATOS
  What's happened to my uncle? Has he died?   680

DAOS
  He didn't die, and he can come to life again.

KLEOSTRATOS
  Daos, what are you saying?
  Are you completely out of your mind?

DAOS
  It was a plot, a plan to save your sister.
  But now you're here and can take care of her.
  Your uncle Smikrines had tried to marry her
  to get his hands on the dowry you'd won.
  We'll tell you more inside, but first we'll tell
  Chairestratos that you've returned.
  You've risen from the dead indeed,   690
  and so shall he, in truth, in fact, today,
  and we shall have no tragedy,
  but Smikrines will rue this day.
*(They both go inside, arm in arm as the Chorus of revelers comes out for
                      the last time.)*

CHORUS
Eros throws his dice on Mount Olympus.
Insane, I try to fight but must concede.
Love has cast his thunderbolts against us
and plays his games with lovely Ganymede.

ACT V

(Daos emerges from Chairestratos' house.)

DAOS
I've never believed that such a scene
existed outside tragi-comedy.
Chairestratos could not believe his eyes.   700
He looked the way I must have looked
when I first saw Kleostratos returned
as from the dead. A double resurrection
has just taken place. A double marriage
soon will follow. The daughter of Chairestratos
will wed Kleostratos, and his sister
will have her Chaireas. The neighbors
have been witnesses, and they are formally
betrothed. What remains is Smikrines.
Chairestratos reluctantly agreed   710
to lie low for a while and let me have
some fun with him. (If I get my freedom
for my pains, I won't be disappointed.)
(Neighbor emerges from Chairestratos' house and approaches Daos.)

NEIGHBOR
Why are you walking about by yourself,
by Zeus? You should be planning the parties.

DAOS
I'll have the cook back soon, and all the servers.
The weddings will take place. Kleostratos is safe,
but needs a bit of rest. By Heracles,
here comes the friend I need, and you can stay

and help us dole out a dollop of justice   720
to our noble elder Smikrines.
(Chaireas' friend Sostratos, the "doctor," arrives .)

SOSTRATOS *(rushing up excitedly)*
I've heard the news, and thanks to Zeus my ruse
no longer is of use. I've come to celebrate.

DAOS
Be patient for a while, put your "doctor" get-up on,
and we can have some fun with Smikrines.
*(Sostratos goes off stage; soon after, Smikrines comes out of his house and
approaches Daos and the neighbor.)*

SMIKRINES
I've come to see my brother's wife and family.
We must grieve and then proceed past grieving.

DAOS
What does that mean?

SMIKRINES
I'm still a man with a plan. Sostratos
can be a witness as I pledge myself   730
to my brother's daughter. Chaireas
will have his due from me. The dowry
that you brought goes with the girl.

DAOS
How kind and conscientious you do seem.
(goes to the edge of the stage and addresses the audience)
His palms are itching, that's for sure, I see.
but partly he's a man to pity.
Oh, they are triply miserably unhappy
who must have more than anybody else.
They guard their forts and hold the heights
and wear themselves thin keeping their own.   740

But just as a dagger can bring down a king,
a bit of fun will flatten Smikrines.
(Sostratos reappears in his "doctor" garb.)

SOSTRATOS *(rushing up excitedly)*
I zink I have found a miracle cure.
Perhaps my papyrus giffs me a clue
which vill vork in cases where
bile bulges out from ascites und ve
must find ze trick to make it go beck.

SMIKRINES *(baffled)*
What are you saying? My brother is dead.

SOSTRATOS
Not until I say he is.
(Sostratos goes into Chairestratos' house.)

DAOS
Perhaps there is hope. Chairestratos may live.   750

SMIKRINES
Try not to get your hopes up, boy.

DAOS *(sarcastically)*
Whose hopes are up? Who hopes for marriages
and every dowry larger than the last?

SMIKRINES *(in anger)*
The mill will wear you out, you Phrygian,
and no friend will protect you. Kleostratos
and my brother are gone, and soon you'll be a goner.

DAOS
Which girl is prettier? When you were palming
the gold, did you notice the mules or the girls
apart from their worth? You don't have enough?

SMIKRINES *(becoming apoplectic)*
>   I'm calling for marshals to take you away.   760
>   Either you're mad or you're worse, you're a curse
>   of an insubordinate slave.

DAOS *(laughing)*
>   Look who's coming out of the house!
*(Smikrines sees Chairestratos, healthy and smiling, emerge with
                  Kleostratos. He grabs onto Daos.)*

SMIKRINES *(in shock and shaking uncontrollably)*
>   My mind is giving out. I can't be seeing
>   what I see. Is that my nephew back
>   from the grave, my brother healthy again?
>   What could that doctor have done?
>   Could he summon up Kleostratos?
>   I never thought that lunacy
>   was ever in our family,   770
>   and yet I must be mad. I must lie down.
>   Daos, help me to my house.
(Daos catches him as he is about to faint and holds him up.)

CHAIRESTRATOS
>   Brother, what you see is real. The gods are good
>   and Chance has been allied to us.
>   My property will someday go
>   to my daughter and Kleostratos,
>   and some to his sister and Chaireas.
>   You may come as a guest to the weddings.
>   I hope this day brings happiness to all.

SMIKRINES *(humiliated and angry)*
>   I'm weak, I'm going home to rest.   780
>   I see you've made a test of me
>   and I'm not in the mood for a party.
>   Go have your fun and stay away.

Go celebrate and stuff yourselves.
But I'm accustomed to be by myself,
and will content myself with what I've got.
(Smikrines makes his unsteady way off stage.)

DAOS *(to Kleostratos)*
Am I really free? I'll enjoy your wedding
as your friend, and ask the audience
to applaud our fortunes and our future.

About the Translators

PALMER BOVIE was educated at the Lawrenceville School and Princeton University. He received his Ph.D. degree in classics from Columbia University and taught at Columbia, Princeton, Indiana University, the American Academy in Rome, and Rutgers University, where he is Emeritus Professor of Classics. He has published many translations from classical literature, including Virgil's *Georgics*, orations of Cicero, satires and epistles of Horace, epigrams of Martial, and the *De rerum natura* of Lucretius. With David R. Slavitt he coedited the Complete Roman Drama in Translation series.

SHEILA D'ATRI is a graduate of Brooklyn College and received her M.A. and Ph.D. degrees in classics from Rutgers University, where she has taught Greek, Latin, Roman civilization, and mythology. An earlier version of her *Dyskolos* appeared in *Classical Comedy: Greek and Roman*, edited by Robert W. Corrigan.

RICHARD ELMAN died in December 1997, as this book was going to press. He was the author of twenty-six books of fiction, poetry, and journalism, including *An Education in Blood, Tar Beach, Homage to Fats Navarro, Disco Frito, Cocktails at Somoza's*, and the novelization of the movie *Taxi Driver*. He published widely in magazines and quarterlies and broadcast reviews and commentary for National Public Radio. He taught at Bennington College, Columbia University, Sarah Lawrence College, the University of Pennsylvania, and elsewhere. In 1990 he was the first creative writer appointed to the Abrams Chair of Jewish Studies at the University of Notre Dame. The recipient of grants from the National Endowment or the Arts and the New York State CAPS, he was visiting professor of creative writing at the State University of New York, Stony Brook.

CPSIA information can be obtained
at www.ICGtesting.com
Printed in the USA
LVOW03s0530031117
554866LV00001B/4/P